# ROPE & RAIL
# NORTHERN ISLES
## Mike Bent

**Front Cover** The shipping jetty at the Sveagruva mine, Svalbard.

*Author's Collection*

**Back Cover** The Tunnel Boring Machine (TBM) and associated narrow gauge railway infrastructure, used on the Eiði 2 Hydro Electric Project in the Faroe Islands.

*Heinrik Hommelgard*

**Above** The remains of the Qullissat Coal Mine Railway on Disko Island, Greenland.

*Klaus Bodholt Andreasen*

Published by Mainline & Maritime Ltd
3 Broadleaze, Upper Seagry, near Chippenham, SN15 5EY
Tel: 07770 748615
www.mainlineandmaritime.co.uk   orders@mainlineandmaritime.co.uk
Printed in the UK
ISBN: 978-1-900340-89-2

# HELGOLAND

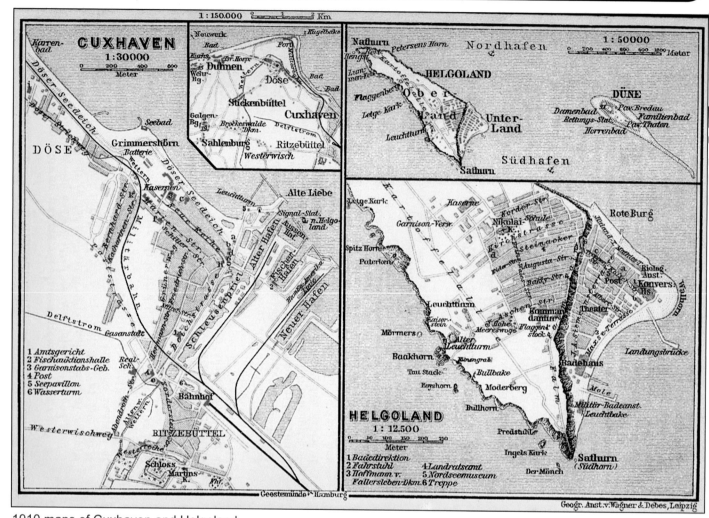

1910 maps of Cuxhaven and Helgoland.

Some 46 km west of Büsum on the North Sea coast are Helgoland and Dune, Germany's only 'deep sea' offshore islands, situated in the Deutsche Bucht, near the Elbe and Weser estuaries and the western end of the Nord-Ostsee Kanal. Their strategic position during the two world wars resulted in both having extensive Feldbahn rail networks, and there are still a few industrial archaeological remains associated with these awaiting discovery by visitors.

The two-island archipelago, situated at 54°11'N, 7°53'E, became an island as sea levels rose following the last Ice Age, between 130,000 and 480,000 years ago. Helgoland distinguishes itself from the other German islands, both in the Baltic and North Sea, on account of its high sandstone cliffs on the west coast. In 325 BC Pliny the Elder reckoned that the explorer Pytheas of Massalia could well have discovered Helgoland on his circumnavigation of Britain, when he is believed to have ventured as far north as the Arctic Circle and possibly also into the Baltic. His discovery of amber (which he said was used instead of firewood by the locals) tends to support his landing either on Helgoland or on what is now the Polish coast north of present-day Gdynia.

The name 'Helgoland' may have been derived from 'Heiligenland' (Holy Land) or from the Frisian word 'Hallaglun' or 'Halligland' - this referring to an island in a salty marsh, periodically covered by the tide.

The island is believed to have been settled from prehistoric times. The population is considered to be ethnic Frisian, and the local dialect of the North Frisian language was still spoken on the island until the late 19th century. Ownership of the island varied – at times it was part of Denmark, at times part of the Duchy of Schleswig-Holstein, and at others the property of the Hanseatic Free City of Hamburg. In 1714 it was seized by Denmark and remained Danish territory until 1807, when under one of the agreements following the Napoleonic Wars it was taken over by Britain. This take-over was ratified under the Treaty of Kiel of 14 January 1814. During Napoleon's continental blockade between 1807 and 1813 it served as a smuggling and espionage base, a channel for the illegal entry to the continent of luxuries such as cotton, coffee, tea and sugar. The islanders enjoyed a brief period of economic prosperity, rather than having to earn their living from fishing. In 1811 Trinity House built the first lighthouse on the island.

The idea of developing Helgoland as a seaside spa (Seebad) was that of the ship's master Jakob Siemens (1794 to 1849). He encountered some opposition to this dea from many of the islanders, but on 6 March 1826 founded a joint stock company, Seebad Helgoland, with 20 100-mark shares. That first summer around 100 visitors were brought to the island in open sailing boats, which took around 12 hours on passage from the mainland. By 1829 the number of visitors had doubled, and that year the Amsterdam-registered paddle steamer *De Beurs van Amsterdam* of the Dutch shipping company Reederei Amsterdamsche Stoombootmaatschapij began services from and to Hamburg. Over 300 visitors to the island were recorded in summer 1830.

*De Beurs van Amsterdam* was built in 1826 by Werf het Roopaard, Corn. van Swieten, Amsterdam. She was of 301 tonnes, 40.3 m long overall, with a beam of 5.73 m and a depth of 3.43 m. Her engines were supplied by Henry Maudslay of London. Originally she was used on a service between Amsterdam and London. On 10 June 1829 she was acquired by Wurfbain & Co. of Hamburg for the Helgoland run. She was withdrawn from service in 1849 and her engines were then installed in another, much larger paddle steamer, *De Stoomvaart*, which was employed on Amsterdam to Hamburg services..

Regular steamer services between Hamburg and Helgoland started up in 1834 following the founding on 28 February 1833 of the Hamburger Dampfschiffahrts Compagnie with a share capital of 90.000 Marks, using the paddle steamer *Elbe*. The first sailing was advertised for 17 May, the second for 21 June.

## The First Railway Era

Helgoland was nominally a British protectorate. Although the British maintained a naval presence there, no attempt was made to look after the island's population, which, composed mainly of farmers and fishermen, started forming closer ties with their German neighbours. To all intents and purposes, during most of the 19th century Helgoland was a German state. The ambiguous state of affairs was reflected on the island's stamps, which showed Queen Victoria's head but were denominated in Hamburg Schillings. The island's strategic position attracted the interest of Kaiser Wilhelm I and Otto von Bismarck after 1871, and following the creation of the German Empire there was renewed interest in gaining possession of the island, to protect German naval bases and commercial shipping entering and leaving the various large ports on the southern shore of the Elbe estuary. The Helgoland-Zanzibar treaty of 1 July 1890 resulted in the German Empire trading some of its colonial interests in Zanzibar and East Africa to Britain, in return for Helgoland, which duly became part of Schleswig-Holstein Land on 10 August 1890.

The new proprietors soon started planning the development of the islands as a major naval and military base, to protect the western end of the recently completed Nord-Ostsee Kanal (Kiel Canal). By February 1891 draft plans had been prepared, and work began the following summer to fortify the upper plateau of Helgoland (known as Oberland), with the creation of several gun emplacements. One vital task was to provide a means of transport linking the plateau with the new quay (the one on which today are the customs offices). Metre gauge track was laid on the quays, and a double track inclined plane built, passing through two short tunnels at its lower and upper ends. Wagons, the ubiquitous four-wheel tipping tubs known as Feldbahnloren, were pushed manually up the steep inclined

An early view of the inclined plane, looking towards the harbour.

*Author's Collection*

plane! North of the upper tunnel the line continued across Oberland to the northern end of the island, with branches to the various gun emplacements. A rail network was developed eastwards from the quay to serve the low-lying Unterland, including the island's power station (situated in the centre of the town) and various workshops.

The first locomotive to arrive on the island was probably a metre gauge Klöckner-Humboldt-Deutz diesel built in 1911, works number 836, for the Kaiserliche Werft, Wilhelmshaven. The same year a 600 mm gauge two-axle electric locomotive was built by Siemens-Schuckert Werke (SSW), works number 700, for Preußisches Wasserbauamt, although its date of arrival on the island is not known. In 1912 SSW supplied two more similar machines, of metre gauge (works numbers 773 and 774) to Artilleriebahn Helgoland. Another 600 mm gauge locomotive, built in 1914 by SSW for Preußisches Wasserbauamt, works number 1,013, could have arrived at the same time as the first one, but certainly before 1918.

The first steam locomotive arrival, in 1917, was a metre gauge 0-6-0T built in 1901 by Freudenstein (works number 68), a metre gauge machine which had started its life on the Sylter Südbahn, and later on the Sylter Inselbahn, where it carried the number 8. There then followed two 0-4-0Ts built by O&K in 1915 (works numbers 6,732 and 6,735). Information and photos are rare - the civilian population was evacuated from Helgoland during the First World War.

An inspection party descends the inclined plane.

These early rail networks were short-lived: following the Treaty of Versailles destruction of the military installations on Helgoland was ordered under the supervision of the Allied Disarmament Commission. The munitions bunkers were partially filled with cement, though mixed so that it would easily crumble for future removal. The tunnels on the inclined plane were reduced in size and the portals blocked. It is not known whether the tracks were lifted. By 1922 the work had been completed, and so ended the first railway era on the island.

## The Second Railway Era

The coming to power of the Nazis in 1933 saw the start of a rearmament policy, this also involving Helgoland and Dune under a tidying-up strategy initially known as 'Aufräumarbeiten auf Helgoland', starting in May 1935. The bunkers were cleared of concrete and the underground network of tunnels and chambers was greatly enlarged (it is now open to visitors), the upper tunnel on the inclined plane was reopened, and the metre gauge network on Oberland was revived. Under Projekt Hummerschere ('Lobster Claw Project') it was planned to create a huge naval base with U-boat pens, the breakwaters extending north from Helgoland and Dune in a pincer-like shape. This involved the reconstruction of sea defences at the foot of the cliffs on the west side of Helgoland, ending at a breakwater north of the 45 m high sandstone stack known as Lange Anna. A breakwater already existed by 1928 along this part of the

coast, and it seems that it was simply rebuilt, a few metres further to the west, to skirt the various headlands. A railway, which appears to have been of 600 mm gauge, was laid alongside this, and was served by a fleet of diesel locomotives built by Diema, hauling Feldbahnloren wagons loaded with construction materials. An airfield was built on low-lying Dune, which by 1941 had been enlarged in size through land reclamation projects, and which also had its own rail network.

Statistics for August 1940 indicate that the motive power and rolling stock fleet on the islands consisted of 22 metre gauge locomotives, 27 of 600 mm gauge (this figure may be dubious), and 602 Loren wagons. Suppliers included Orenstein & Koppel (14 between 1937 and 1940), Klöckner-Humboldt-Deutz (seven between 1939 and 1941), Schöma (four in 1939 and 1940), Henschel (four in 1940) and Jung (one, from the Rendsburger Kleinbahn, later moved to the Sylter Inselbahn, in the early 1940s, and in 1945 returned to the Rendsburger Kleinbahn). One of the Deutz diesels was 600 mm gauge, and was delivered in 1941 to Hinz & Köhring, a construction company on Helgoland. Freight was moved in a fleet of 602 Loren wagons.

The stretches of line are listed by the Deutsche Gesellschaft für Eisenbahngeschichte (German Railway History Society) as:

7.1818.001  1823  Helgoland, Mole - Oberland Nord
7.1818.002  1824  Helgoland, Westmole - Nordmole

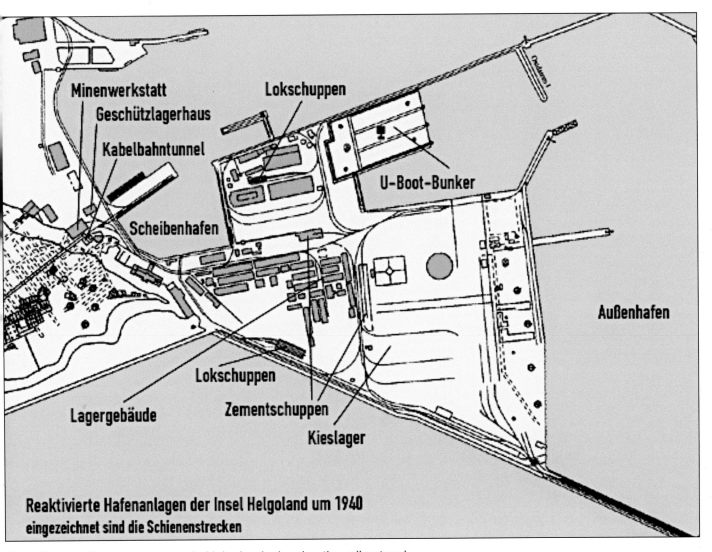

A 1940 map of the harbour area in Helgoland, showing the rail network.

*Author's Collection*

An artist's impression published in the British newspaper 'The Sphere' immediately after the end of the Second World War, showing the military installations, but not, unfortunately, the railways..

*The Sphere Archive, Author's Collection*

7.1818.006 2150 Helgoland, Transportbahn Westmauer des preuß. Wasserbauamtes

7.1818.007 2151 Helgoland, Artilleriebahn Geschützstellungen Nordspitze

7.1818.008 2152 Helgoland, Artilleriebahn zu Geschützstellungen im Südhafen mit Spitzkehre

7.1818.009 1828 Helgoland, Transportbahn von 1955 (no longer in use)

The first number is the DGEG code, the second is the official line identification code.

Naturally, the archipelago was a prime target for Allied bombing campaigns. A major bombardment involving 969 aircraft on 18 April 1945, the day the civilian population (around 3,000) was evacuated, resulted in the destruction of a large part of the rail network. Afterwards the system remained out of use, with looters stealing locomotives, rolling stock and rails. The looters must have risked their lives, since the RAF and Royal Navy continued the bombardments after the end of the war, in an endeavour to destroy all the military installations – and a fair part of the civilian settlements on Oberland and Unterland as well.

The bombing culminated in 'Operation Big Bang' on 18 April 1947, the subterranean bunkers, U-boat pens and other installations having been primed with around 6,700 tonnes of high explosives, all detonated remotely from RN vessels some 14 km distant at 13.00 that day. The lighthouse and a tall control tower survived the blasts – and so did an old grey rabbit, called Rupert, who had been observed during the days prior to the explosion by the teams of demolition workers, and who had deviously evaded the traps set to capture him and thus move him to safety. Following one of the largest single non-nuclear detonations in history he was observed hopping around safe and sound by a team of military visitors. A video of the explosion can be found at https://www.youtube.com/watch?v=LtatVS-Tk3c.

It was not until 20 December 1950 that René Leudesdorff and Georg von Hatzfeld, two students from Heidelburg University, together with Professor Hubertus zu Löwenstein, became the first civilians to re-occupy Helgoland and raise German and local flags there. They were arrested by the British military, but their action sparked off a campaign to rehabilitate the island, clear undetonated ammunition (though unexploded bombs have been found as recently as 2013), and rebuild the settlements on Unterland and Oberland. The former inhabitants were allowed to return on 1 March 1952.

Of the railway remains, the most prominent is the upper part of the inclined plane, now a concrete road, passing through the upper tunnel, of much reduced loading gauge, and used mainly by electric freight vehicles (the only hydrocarbon-fuelled vehicles on the island are the ambulance and police van!). At the top end of the tunnel there is, incredibly, a short stretch of 600 mm gauge track. All traces of the lower end of the inclined plane, and of the lower tunnel, have now disappeared, obliterated by the 'Big Bang' - though recent photographs show a fragment of rock wall which may have been the parapet of the upper portal of the lower tunnel. Until recently there were also some

Helgoland in 1988. The lower end of the inclined plane has disappeared as a result of the bombing which created 'Mittelland' The upper portal of the lower tunnel was probably situated just this side of the sharp curve in the road.
*Bundesanstalt für Wasserbau archives*

stretches of dual gauge track on the southern quays, but this area is now being redeveloped as part of a wind farm project. The breakwater along the foot of the cliffs on the spectacular west coast still exists, but all traces of the railway have disappeared, the concrete topping being of recent application. Similarly, there are no vestiges of the line which once traversed Oberland – following the war the area was pitted with bomb craters, many of which still exist.

Of the various locomotives used on the island, there is one known survivor. This is Deutz 36708, which following the war was moved to Wangerooge, then to the Inselbahn Spiekeroog. In 1969 it was acquired by the Deutscher Eisenbahnverein of Bruchhausen-Vilsen (not far from Bremen), whence the society operates a 7.8 km metre gauge line to Heiligenberg and Asendorf. It is currently plinthed on the east side of Harlesiel ferry terminal, the former station, on the mainland south of Spiekeroog.

## Access

Gone are the days of the Hamburg to Helgoland and Bremen to Helgoland shipping services operated by the likes of *Wappen von Hamburg* (1965) and *Roland von Bremen* (1939, formerly J. Lauritzen's *Indian Reefer*). Gone also is the lovely *Atlantis* of 1972, sold in early 2016 to a company in the Seychelles. Nowadays the islands can be accessed via the ports of Büsum (April to November), Cuxhaven (year-round), Hookseil (special sailings) and Bremerhaven (May to September), crossing times varying between 2h30 and 3h. The operator is Adler & Eils, the result of the recent merger (early 2019) between Alder and Reederei Cassen Eils (for fare and timetable details see www.adler-eils.de), using an interesting fleet of passenger ships. The most recent is the magnificent 2.256 gt. *Helgoland*, which entered service in summer 2017. *Funny Girl* (999 gt.), dating from 1973 and named after the 1968 film which starred Barbara Streisand and Omar Sharif, was refitted in 2017 to offer a similar accommodation standard to her new running-mate. The fleet's veteran is *Fair Lady*, (935 gt.1970), named after the 1964 film starring Audrey Hepburn and Rex Harrison). Rather smaller (406 gt.) is *Flipper* of 1977 (presumably named after the 1963 film).

**Above:** The only motorised road vehicles allowed on Helgoland nowadays are electric ones, apart from the police van and ambulance. This e-vehicle is emerging from the upper tunnel on the inclined plane on 28 September 2014.

**Right:** The only surviving rails known to exist on Helgoland nowadays, at the northern exit from the upper tunnel. This photo dates from 28 September 2014.

**Below:** The view from the quayside looking towards the inclined plane and tunnel on 28 September 2014.

*All: Author*

# SVALBARD

This view of Longyearbyen features a ropeway on the skyline, a cable-hauled incline, and a conventional railway in the foreground - an industrial archaeologist's paradise.

In *Locomotives International* Issue 116 readers visited Ny-Ålesund to investigate the history of Europe's northernmost railway, and almost certainly one of the northernmost rail-based transport systems in the world. Yet the Svalbard archipelago was also home to many more unusual railways built around the turn of the 19th and 20th centuries, when the world powers politely vied with one another for control over this icy, mineral-rich No Man's Land...

## The Summer of '74 . . .

The author visited Longyearbyen travelling on board Det Nordenfjeldske Dampskibsselskab's *Harald Jarl*, on the weekly Svalbard-Express in early August 1974. In those days the Hurtigrute companies maintained this service using four of their most recent ships, together with the 1956-built *Nordstjernen*. Cruise liners did occasionally visit the archipelago, but the small size of the Hurtigrute vessels, all under around 2,500 gt., and their ice-strengthened hulls made them ideal for inshore work and calling at the small

quays at Longyearbyen and Ny-Ålesund.

The Svalbard-Express was promoted using a page within the standard summer version of the Hurtigrute brochure. Rather than opt for the expensive first class package, which was the one always targeted at foreign tourists, I first wrote to Det Bergenske Dampskibsselskab's London office to find out about ordinary second class fares, and managed to secure for myself a second class single fare on the company's 1952-built *Polarlys* from Bergen to Kirkenes, and back to Honningsvåg, the fare, if I recall correctly, being somewhere between 50 and 60 pounds sterling(!), this including a berth in a twin-berth cabin on the shelter deck, aft, but no food. The price of on-board cafeteria food sent many like-minded travellers searching in the shops and supermarkets at ports of call for cheaper alternatives. Meals and snacks thus became picnics on deck! BDS also offered me a second class fare from Honningsvåg via Svalbard and back to Bergen on board *Harald Jarl*, again in a twin-berth second class cabin on 'C' deck (the lowest), but this time with all meals included, this costing around 110

An August 1974 view of one of the aerial ropeways at Longyearbyen, looking southeast up Adventfjorden.

*Author*

pounds sterling. Even at 1974 prices, this fare worked out as an excellent bargain. Once you saw the quality and quantity of food served in the second class dining saloon, starboard side, amidships, just abaft the first class restaurant, it was evident that this was indeed a remarkable bargain - it was the same fare as that served to those travelling first class. All passengers booking to Svalbard, regardless of class, were provided with full board and lodgings. Full board, by the way, consisted of a buffet breakfast, buffet lunch, and a three-course evening meal (with second and third helpings of each course, until the food ran out) with tea or coffee afterwards. The buffets were Norwegian style, in other words, sumptuous. And at 18 years of age I had a huge appetite!

Having disembarked from *Polarlys* early in the morning at a chilly and misty Honningsvåg (Tuesday, a week after leaving Bergen) I had a full day to explore locally on foot, enabling me to have a mid-morning wander on board BDS's northbound *Nordstjernen*, for which I have rather a fondness, since she was built in the same year that I left the maternal slipway. She is now part of the Norwegian national heritage collection. I doubt whether I could achieve that ranking!

*Harald Jarl* arrived on her limited-stop sailing from Bergen in the early evening, her passengers then joining a bus for their Nordkapp excursion, and we sailed an hour before midnight, thus enabling us to be off Nordkapp at the moment the midnight sun brushed the northern horizon. We reached Bjørnøya in the early afternoon of Wednesday, a filthy cold, misty, windy day, and proceeded up the west coast to Bjørnøya Radio, where supplies (reputedly

including a batch of porno films) were landed using an inflatable boat belonging to the lonely radio and meteorological team. The mist persisted until after we had called at Isfjord Radio early on Thursday morning (here a most strange floating contraption was used for taking supplies ashore), and then, as we headed further up Isfjorden everything cleared miraculously, and we were blessed with a brilliant summer's day!

Programming over the three days spent in Svalbard was rather ad-hoc, dependent on weather, cargo and ice conditions. Nevertheless, it was amazing what it was possible to fit in, although nights became rather sleepless. Thursday's lunch was an undignified scramble before we were herded on board the northernmost full-size bus in the world for a brisk drive up Longyeardalen to the end of the hardcore road, followed by a scramble up the side moraine at the snout of the glacier, for a stroll on the rapidly melting ice. This shore excursion (unlike those on the coastal Hurtigrute for second class passengers) was provided free of charge for all! Once up on the moraines, most folk busied themselves collecting fossils. Only a few of us ventured any distance onto the rather soggy ice, and to return decided to descend over the glacier's snout, getting our feet soaked in the icy meltwater stream at the base. Our shoes and socks soon dried off on the long hike back to the ship, through Longyearbyen village, having missed the return bus!

My photography in those days involved the use of slow-exposure Kodachrome 25 ASA film, fed into a secondhand Yashica camera, secured a few weeks before the voyage for a bargain 25 pounds, and which served me faithfully until the day in 2007 when I bought my first digital camera, when the wind-on mechanism jammed solid. It had out-lived its Japanese manufacturer by two years! But Kodachrome film was expensive, even in 1974, about 2.20 pounds per 36-exposure roll, and even with ten of these one had to ration one's photography - some things have indeed changed for the better. But looking at these photos 45 years later the quantity of industrial artefacts which existed in Svalbard in 1974 was fairly impressive - from the remains of the railway and rusting steam locomotive at Ny-Ålesund to the ropeways still active at Longyearbyen, and the railway viaduct near the head of Longyeardalen, just below the snout of the glacier.

We sailed from Longearbyen in mid-evening that Thursday, weighted down by considerable additions to the cargo (yes, fossils) in many of the passengers' cabins. The fresh water tanks had been filled with glacier meltwater, which gave the drinking water in the restaurant a slightly cloudy appearance. A group of Norwegians returning home had just received their August alcohol ration (cans of beer). These were generously shared around in the second class cafeteria  and the party went on until the wee hours of Friday, by which time we were off the northwest coast of Prins Karls Forland. Time seemed to have stopped - it was 02.00, the sun was high in the sky, and we were all just that slightest bit tipsy. A Norwegian drinking song competition ended up with *Harald Jarl*'s third officer being doused in beer. I must confess to a longstanding liking for beer. My mother had been home-brewing the stuff (and it was powerful, too), since the late 1960s. She was also an expert at producing mind-blowing home-made wines. Homework was regularly done in an alcoholic haze. No harm done, as far as I am aware . . .

After a brief nap, we were all on deck again early on an overcast Friday morning awaiting our first glimpse of the pack ice, through which we nosed cautiously, some 500 miles from the North Pole. 'If you want to go any further, you will have to walk', we were informed.

Somewhere beyond 80°N, the coast out of sight to the southeast, *Harald Jarl* swung round, left the ice, and headed for Magdalenefjorden. Now, if you log onto the Norsk Polarinstitutt's excellent Toposvalbard cartography website, and look at some recent photos, you will see that, tragically, Magdalenefjorden is but a shadow of its former self, anthropogenic global warming to blame. Gone are the blue ice-cliffs, the glaciers have retreated, and there is much dark bare rock.

It might be worth mentioning that on board *Harald Jarl* we were allowed the free run of the ship, from stem to stern, literally, and including the bridge wings and wheelhouse. How privileged we were, compared with most 'cruise' passengers nowadays . . . On this occasion, while we were at rest in Magdalenefjorden,  a lifeboat was lowered with a professional photographer aboard, to take some photos for the following year's Hurtigrute brochure. By 1975 one of these photos had been duly framed and was hanging in the purser's office on board *Harald Jarl*.

From Magdalenefjorden we closely followed the coast, in those days fringed with fairly long stretches of ice cliffs at the ends of glaciers, to Kongsfjorden and Ny-Ålesund, where we were welcomed by the settlement's 'Slag og Blæse Ensemble 79°N'. This curious little musical ensemble ('Puff and Wind' is the translation) has survived into the 21st century, reflecting the tradition in many Norwegian towns of having brass bands, and greets most arriving and departing ships with its dulcet, harmonious melodic notes and amazingly strict timing. For a sample, relax to https://www.youtube.com/watch?v=QUFEuX8g3pM...    Another even more interesting performance can be heard on https://www.nrk.no/troms/tonedovt-band-sender-turister-bort-1.8259362

The free beer was still flowing as we headed south that evening, and the sun was shining high in the sky again at 02.00. Early on Saturday morning - bleary-eyed and before breakfast - we found ourselves deep in Tempelfjorden, an inner arm of Isfjorden, about to make a turn off Tunabreen, before passing close under the spectacular cliffs of Templet (Temple Mountain). An unexpected 'extra' on this cruise full of 'extras'.

We were back in Longyearbyen shortly after breakfast, and heeding warnings not to venture onto the glacier again unless accompanied by a guide, ventured off on independent exploration. Somehow, in the early 1970s, industrial transport systems failed to arouse the interest that they do now - perhaps because they were rather more commonplace in those days! More fascinating were the miners' barracks, with all piped domestic facilities - water, sewage and heating - encased in wood and carried above ground level, on account of the permafrost.

The weather remaining fine, after lunch we continued west from Longyearbyen, hugging the coast, passing the abandoned Russian mining settlement of Grumantbyen. Thin smoke was rising from among the ruins, and close to the shoreline there was what appeared to be a very long wooden box. This, presumably, was a snowshed for the mineral railway between the coal mines and the quay in Colesbukta.

Our final bit of exploration involved a venture up Grønfjorden, passing close to the Russian mining village of Barentsburg, home nowadays of the only active mineral railway on the archipelago. Here, a large collier and a steam tug were moored at the quay. And finally, back to Isfjord Radio to collect the mail, and out into the mist, bound for Bjørnøya, Tromsø and Bergen.

Let us now review the various mining settlements, both extant and extinct, which had, or still have rail-based transport systems. We start in the centre of the largest island in the archipelago,. Spitsbergen, on the shores of Isfjorden, the largest fjord system, with Svalbard's oldest railway . . .

## Svenskehus and its Railway

Svenskehuset ('the Swedish House') is the only large 19th century building still remaining in Svalbard, and is protected under the archipelago's Environmental Law. A major restoration took place in 1982, including wall and roof repairs. The building is situated near Kapp Thordsen, a headland on the northern side of Isfjorden, with Nordfjorden on its west side and Billejorden on its east side. In 1864 a Swedish expedition led by Adolf Erik Nordenskiöld undertook a geological survey of the district, discovering coprolite (fossilised animal dung). This, once treated with sulphuric acid, had commercial potential, since the phosphate content could be extracted and used as a fertiliser. At that time the East Anglian Fens in Cambridgeshire and the Isle of Ely were the main coprolite mining area in the world, refining being undertaken in Ipswich by Fisons.

In winter 1871/2 the Norwegian/Swedish state authorities

decided to establish a residential colony in Isfjorden to support the newly founded Isfjorden AB, whose intention was to exploit the coprolites, undertake wintertime hunting, perform Arctic research, and develop an incipient tourism trade in summer. Leading the project for the first two years was Johan Tiberg, from northern Norway, whose wife, Sofie, was Swedish, with his son Johan Petter (then 16) and daughter Jacobine, six. It was envisaged that several families would overwinter. An office was established in Tromsø for the hiring of miners and colonists.

A large house was built in summer 1872, the prefabricated parts being brought from Göteborg. Some exploratory work took place nearby for coprolites, but these were found to occur in too small a quantity for economic exploitation. Once removed from the permafrost, they were found to contain phosphate mixed with earth and stone. This would make mining in winter difficult. Moreover, the landing conditions on the coast there were rather difficult. A 600 m long cable had to be run out from the shore and attached to the winches of visiting steamships. The cable and winches were used to move lighters between the shore and ship. But the system could only be used in calm conditions. At the end of August the project was wound up, and Isfjorden AB was liquidated. The house was left abandoned, but well stocked with food and hunting supplies, and all that was necessary for overwintering. The management of Isfjorden AB asked the Norwegian State to make the house available for overwintering hunting parties in need of shelter.

The history of what subsequently became known as the Svenskehus then took a grim turn. In September 1872 Adolf Eril Nordenskiöld established a polar research station at Mosselbukta, in the north of the archipelago, at the mouth of Wijdefjorden. The research team consisted of 28 people, and had three steamers for use, *Onkel Adam*, *Gladan* and *Polheim*. Of these, *Polheim* was to overwinter with the research team, and the other two were to return south as soon as the weather started to deteriorate. An enclosure was made to house captured reindeer, which were castrated and ear-marked.

On the evening of 15 September a farewell party was held at the base for those who were to return to Norway the following day. During the evening the wind turned northerly, and increased in strength, becoming a full gale overnight. Dawn revealed that Widjefjorden was iced over, the temperature having plummeted to -29°C. All three steamers were trapped. In addition to the 28 members of the research team, 37 other men and one woman (the first woman believed to have overwintered in Svalbard) were now trapped on board the steamers. The woman was Amanda Wenneberg, the cook on board *Onkel Adam*.

During the storm four whalers/sealers from the Tromsø fleet sought shelter at Gråhuken, the headland on the west shore of Widjefjorden, near its mouth and became trapped in the ice. A similar fate befell two vessels at Velkomstpynten, the next headland to the west, on the

In this image of the Svenskehus, the small building is little more than a dot in the centre of a landscape dominated by the scars of early mining operations.
*Bjoertvedt via Wikimedia Commons*

western shore of Woodfjorden. On all six vessels there were 58 men. By early October in all 124 people were faced with the prospects of overwintering on the archipelago, with insufficient food supplies either on shore or on the ships for all of them. Those vessels which had left the mainland in May had supplies for five months, and by late September on-board provisions were beginning to run low.

Seven of the men from the trapped vessels managed to walk 40 km over the ice to Mosselbukta, to ask Nordenskiöld for help. He directed them to Kapp Thordsen, where he reckoned there was sufficient food for all. First, he gave them advice on how to avoid getting scurvy. He then prepared a written contract, under which the owners of the vessels would be sent a bill from the Swedish State for the food and supplies consumed at the Svenskehus. In return, the hunters undertook to make a detailed account of their consummations, and also prepare daily weather reports, including wind speed and temperature.

The expedition from Mosselbukta to Kapp Thordsen set out on 7 October with a team of 17 men dragging two boats. They soon found that overnighting on the ice surrounding West-Spitsbergen resulted in them being moved further to the east and north, away from their goal. They thus decided each evening to drag the boats up onto the shore. At noon on 14 October they found themselves in Isfjorden, and off Kapp Thordsen, where they made their base at the Svenskehus.

Soon afterwards, the two vessels trapped at Velkomspynten freed themselves from the ice, and having collected the crews trapped at Gråhuken sailed for Tromsø. Two men, Johannes Matillas from Tromsø and Gabriel Andersen from Kristiansund, were left to look after the remaining vessels, but they both survived, on a poor diet, until the end of April 1873. Of Nordenskiöld's research team, only one person died, paradoxically, of scurvy.

At Svenskehuset hunting of fox, bear and reindeer continued until 29 October, eight beasts being killed. Surplus meat was salted and barrelled. On 2 December Niels Christian Larden from Helgeland fell ill, and by Christmas all 17 men were suffering. Tønnes Gabriel Pedersen from Vest-Agder and the expedition leader,

Henrik Henruiksen, died on 19 January 1873 and were buried in graves 540 m from the house. Sunlight returned briefly on 20 February, and was followed by a spell of good weather, but by then all the men were too sick to make use of it. Three more men died on 19 April. Ulrik Armonsen was the last survivor, and he died in mid-June. The bodies were found on 16 June by skipper Ole Barth Tellefsen from Koppervik, of the Bergen-registered steamer *Elida*, which was on a reindeer hunting expedition.

It was believed for many years that the occupants of the Svenskehus died of scurvy, but in 2008 their graves were opened for posthumous analysis of the remains, this revealing that their bone tissue had a very high lead content, 102.05 microgrammes per gramme, which had apparently accumulated rapidly. This suggested acute lead poisoning.

And finally, what of the railway? This dated from 1882, when a Swedish meteorological expedition overwintered at Kapp Thordsen. The Svenskehus was extended on its south side by a workshop and a new entrance, and several small buildings were erected for storage of scientific equipment. A 900 m long railway (presumably similar to the types found on the Faroe archipelago) was built from the shore to the house, to move supplies. This was the first of many railways to be built on Svalbard.

## Advent City

Søren Zachariassen was born in 1837 in Tromsø, first went to sea at the age of 18, and in 1862 was skipper of the whaler *Prøven*, which ran aground in Isfjorden and was lost. The crew managed to row ashore in the vicinity of present-day Longyearbyen on the western shore of Adventfjorden. Adventfjorden was named after a Hull-registered whaler, *Adventure*, owned by Whitwell, which was there in 1656. While he and the crew were awaiting rescue, Zachariassen rowed north across Isfjorden to Bohemanneset, at the entrance to Nordfjorden. While ashore there he found several lumps of coal, and brought them back with him. It was something that he never forgot...

In 1899 Zachariassen returned to Adventfjorden on board his sloop *Gottfred*, where his crew managed to collect some 56.7m³ of coal from Bohemanneset. This (claimed) first-ever cargo of coal from the archipelago was taken back to Tromsø, where it was sold for 8,837.75 kroner, some to the Macks brewery, some to the local electricity company for power station use, and some to Prince Albert I of Monaco for his steam yacht *Princesse Alice II*, which that year had run aground in Raudfjorden, and had been obliged to put in to Tromsø for repairs.

Zachariassen also gave some coal samples to the skipper Henrik Næss from Trondheim. Næss, together with Oluf Mads Olsen, created a syndicate to investigate further the coal reserves on the shores of Adventfjorden. The following summer they travelled to Svalbard on board the schooner *Depenten*, skippered by Oluf Mads Olsen, and in mid-July claimed mining rights on an area covering 178,556 km², bounded on the south by Colesbukta and on the west by Isfjorden. They started mining in the vicinity of Hotellneset, on the west shore of Adventfjorden, sinking a shaft through 40 feet of fossil ice, using blasting techniques, to reach solid rock. A further 20 feet of sinking resulted in the discovery of a 10-foot thick coal seam. The mining area was fenced in on 25 July 1900 using iron poles and rope (literally 'staking the claim'). The pioneering miners sailed

from Adventfjorden on 15 August bound for Norway with samples of coal, subsequently forming a company, Trondhjem-Spitsbergen Kulkompani, to work the seam.

In 1900 Zachariassen, now having founded the Oslo-based Kulgrubekompaniet Isefjord Spitsbergen with a capital of 1,000 kroner, returned to Adventfjorden on *Gottfred*. They found, to their surprise, that they had been pipped at the post by Næss. Undeterred, Zachariasen apparently made two return trips to Svalbard that summer, to establish his position. He built a house at Bohamanneset with sufficient accommodation for up to 16 men. The building still exists today, in a good state of repair.

Over the following years Albert I of Monaco acted as Zachariassen's patron, providing him with 2,000 kroner and organising four expeditions to Svalbard in 1906 and 1907 using *Princesse Alice II* to chart the archipelago and make meteorological observations. These expeditions led to the forming of a Svalbard research institute (Norsk Svalbardforskningen), which eventually became the Oslo-based Norsk Polarinstutt.

Zachariassen also gave some coal samples to Bernhard Pedersen of Tromsø, who founded another mining company in Bergen, A/S Bergen-Spitsbergen Kulkompani. This discovered coal measures on the northeast shore of Adventfjorden, about 5 km north of the present site of Longyearbyen, and in 1904 sold its mining rights to an English company – the Sheffield-based Spitsbergen Coal and Trading Company (SCTC), which had been founded in London on 23 June that year, one of the founders being William Black of the City of Sheffield Colliery. Shares were issued to the value of 1,969 pounds sterling, half of the shareholders being Norwegians. Most of the British shareholders were from the Sheffield area, and included industrialists, accountants, surveyors, solicitors, estate agents and chartered accountants, as well as 'two married women'. All were enthusiastic to chance their investments in what was by all appearances a very risky mining venture. And since Svalbard was still a No Man's Land, mining there was free from the growing amount of irksome health and safety legislation (and its associated costs) being imposed in Europe. There was no requirement to pay any national or local taxes, or royalties, and the attractiveness of having a non-unionised workforce was also tempting.

Over the first few years SCTC built a barracks for miners, more than 12 sturdily constructed log houses, and a suction producer gas-fuelled power station, whose engines were provided by The Campbell Gas Engine Co. Ltd, of Halifax, Yorkshire. Thus was used to provide electric light, and since it had a short start-up time, of just 15 minutes, it would appear to have been an ideal choice for the location. The manufacturer stated in its brochures that the equipment could also be used with coke, anthracite, timber and even rubbish, so locally-occurring types of fuel could thus have been used. A mine adit was driven into the mountainside, 47 or 48 m above sea level, the working accessed by means of a double track gravity-operated inclined plane, the tracks (possibly of 600 mm gauge, judging from photos) supported on wooden trestles, to keep them clear of snow, descending onto the jetty, which was in an exposed position, open to the northwest and the full length of Isfjorden. Archaeological investigations suggest that initially a basic form of ropeway was used to move coal, until the inclined plane had been completed.

Mining started in 1904, though that year there was still only one barracks to accommodate the workers, a mix of between 30 and 40 Swedes and Norwegians. The mining was straightforward, the coal strata being uncomplicated and easily accessible. The fact that the adit was driven in permafrost eliminated any problems of water seepage and the need for pumping. Pit props were not so essential as in mines in ground which never froze. By way of comparison with many coal mines in Germany, France and England, it was reckoned that the work on Svalbard was easy. But the exceptionally dry air increased the risk of explosions caused by coal dust. There was also the problem of the jetty being unsuitable for use by larger vessels, and the miners' morale dropped during the long Polar winter night. Transport costs were also exceptionally high. Vessels had to sail to Svalbard in ballast, their only cargoes consisting of mining equipment and food supplies.

The first few years were spent developing Advent City, initially two streets, the log-built barracks, and a bakery, the inclined plane and the jetty. In summer 1905 around 200 tonnes of coal were mined. In 1905/6 for the first time, around 30 men overwintered there, with 600 tonnes of coal being mined during the winter, and in 1906/7 no fewer than 70 men endured the long winter, though now with the facilities including a clubhouse and bar to make life more agreeable. The mining results were less productive than anticipated, and there were conflicts between the British management and the international team of miners over the low wages and poor accommodation. We shall return to the tragic story of the STCT later . . .

In 1901 the shipowner Christian Michelsen, who in 1905 was to become the first Norwegian Prime Minister, financed an expedition to Svalbard, and built a house at what is now known as Camp Morton on Van Mijenfjorden, the northern arm of Bellsundet, which runs parallel to and to the south of Isfjorden. The expedition involved some 15,000 USD of investment. Mining possibilities were investigated, with the conclusion that the cost of working the fuel was too high, and its quality was extremely poor. That, one would have thought, would have been sufficient to deter other investors. Surprisingly, it was not... Michelsen's house survives, but needs renovation.

## Mining Revival! Enter John Munroe Longyear

The history of mining on Svalbard was now about to take a momentous turn. In summer 1901 the Hamburg-Amerikanische Packetfahrt-Actien-Gesellschaft's *Auguste Victoria* made a cruise to Nordkapp and Svalbard. On board was John Munroe Longyear, with his wife, Mary, and daughters Abby, Helen and Judith, and sons Jack and Robert. Longyear, born on 15 April 1850, was a developer of timber and mineral concessions in the Upper Peninsula of Michigan, having accumulated a fortune though these activities.

The first stop on the Svalbard cruise itinerary was Bellsundet, at lunchtime on 14 July. Here passengers were taken ashore in the ship's boats. Accompanied by Jack, Longyear headed for the glacier, and scrambled to the top of the end moraine. He observed:

*'The rock in the glacial debris seemed to be slate and slate-conglomerate, with much quartz. It looks to me like a gold country. There was a small vessel in the Sound and the pilot told me that the men in it were prospecting for gold. Spitsbergen now belongs to no country, and if coal or gold are found here some nation will hasten to colonize it.'*

Coincidentally, during the summer of 1901 huge iron ore lodes were discovered in the Sør-Varanger district of eastern Finnmark. The mining area was staked out by Christian Anker, who entered into negotiation with William D. Munroe, a mining engineer who was John Longyear's cousin. One possible argument in favour of exploiting these was that there were coal seams on Andøya in Vesterålen, but these were gas coals, and unsuitable for the processing of iron ore. Anker informed Munroe that this was no real problem, since there were 'unlimited quantities of coal', suitable for this purpose, not far away – on Svalbard.

Longyear consulted with his associate, Frederick Ayer of Boston. Cousin William Munroe had secured an option to buy the mining rights in Sør-Varanger for 18 million kroner, and Longyear was interested in the possibilities of Svalbard for coal. He planned to leave America in mid-June 1903 and travel first to Svalbard, then to deal with the question of Syd-Varagerfjord.

Longyear sailed from Hoboken on 18 June 1903 on board HAPAG's *Auguste-Victoria*, with William Munroe and his associate, Olaus Jeldness (a Norwegian mining engineer with American and Canadian experience) joining at Hammerfest. They arrived off Svalbard on 11 July, first calling at Bellsund and Recherchebukta. On arrival in Adventfjorden at 23.00 that day, they were unable to anchor on account of the gale force conditions. The following morning the wind dropped, permitting anchoring and shore visits. Jeldness and Longyear went off on separate walking expeditions, Jeldness returning in the evening having discovered quantities coal on the shoreline. They remained at Adventfjorden for 36 hours, and managed to make a number of surveys and calculations.

The results of iron ore research in Sør-Varanger were initially not very satisfactory. The ore content was only 42% iron on average, and briquetting would be necessary before subjecting it to a furnace. This, on a large scale, had never before been attempted commercially. Longyear was certain that better ore was available near where he lived in Michigan.

Upon his return to America, Longyear subjected his coal samples to analyses, which were satisfactory, to the extent that he and Ayer started negotiations with the Trondhjem-Spitsbergen Kulkompagni for taking over their mining claims. This latter company had recently forecast that its mines could yield up to 460 million tonnes of coal. It stated that the seams were located between 170 and 180 m above sea level on the southwest side of Adventfjorden. Scree covered most of the mountainsides and tended to freeze solid at very little depth. While transport to the shore (or a jetty) would be easy, using a ropeway, it was reckoned that labour costs would be high and working conditions difficult.

The strategic value of America becoming involved in mining in Svalbard was also noted. In 1903 the USA was challenging Russia over the invasion of Manchuria, and an armed conflict was anticipated. In correspondence Olaus Jeldness observed:

*'We can, for instance, show our country how to attack Russia in the rear by annexing Spitsbergen, and thereby securing an unlimited coal supply and thereby enabling our men of war to reach the White Sea, one of Russia' greatest grain and lumber shipping ports, in thirty hours' sailing. Every statesman in Norway and Sweden knows that Russia is waiting for an opportunity to seize an open port on the Atlantic, and they consider it only a question of time till she takes Norway. If our undertaking results in the annexation of Spitsbergen, Russia's advance on Norway will be*

*blocked, and an untold blessing will be conferred on Scandinavia.'*

On 21 January 1904 the Trondhjem-Spitsbergen Kulkompagni offered Olaus Jeldness an option to purchase its assets, the sale deadline being 1 January 1905. The assets were valued at 350,000 kroner. During 1904 Jeldness and his representatives would have the exclusive right to take possession of the mine workings and all assets on site. If any improvements were made that year to the buildings and infrastructure, should the sale not go through, the Trondhjem-based company reserved the right to take possession of these.

Longyear and Jeldness reckoned that the deal was an attractive one. The considerable thickness of the coal seams meant that mining could continue for hundreds of years before the workings were exhausted. There were also some very significant shareholders in the mining venture. One was the general manager of the Trondhjem-based shipping company NFDS (Det Nordenfjeldske Dampskibsselskab). Another was the manager of the State-owned railway company NSB. A third was the manager of the Rørøs copper mines. Two other large Norwegian shipping companies were also interested in Svalbard coal.

Interest was also growing among the iron ore mining companies in northern Sweden, in the Kiruna and Gällivare districts. Since it was impossible to process iron ore using either charcoal (from vegetation) or from the gas coal found on Andøya, it would be necessary to use imported coal from England, or Norwegian peat. Luossavaara-Kiirunavaara Aktiebolag (LKAB) was founded in 1890, but had subsequently not developed beyond being a mining concern, the ore being sent by rail to Narvik and Luleå for export. Commercial iron ore mining in Sør-Varanger, near Kirkenes at Bjørnevatn, was dependent on the need for local processing facilities (requiring the use of coal) for the ore, thus enhancing its added value, and this did not start until 1910. Northern Norway and Sweden were, in terms of minerals, the richest parts of Scandinavia. One interested company had indicated that it would buy at least 60,000 tonnes of Svalbard coal per annum.

An interesting piece of real estate was the hotel built in the late 1890s by the shipping company VDS (Det Vesteraalske Dampskibsselskab) of Stokmarknes at Hotellneset. This had been originally intended for use in conjunction with cruises operated by the company from Norway, but had now been left abandoned for a couple of years, and was boarded up. The Trondhjem-Spitsbergen Kulkompagni bought it, then sold it separately to Longyear, for 8,000 kroner.

In spring 1905 Jeldness and William Munroe went to Norway to start developing the Arctic Coal Company's mining area on Svalbard. The claims staked were on the opposite side of Adventfjorden to those of the SCTC, and covered land in what was then known as Longyear Valley (now Longyeardalen), running southwest from the fjord with a glacier at its head. The presence of the SCTC worried Longyear. He was a teetotaller, and in Advent City the liquor flowed freely, with inevitable consequences. He also reckoned that the SCTC had invested too heavily in capital equipment, given the poor quality of the coal it extracted. But the SCTC had one important asset. It had recently chartered a 900-tonne steamer to take miners to Svalbard. Munroe, in search of a suitable vessel, expressed an interest in using her. However, he soon discovered that the SCTC was run by a 'Norwegian Englishman' who was a lazy drunkard and bore such a bad reputation that it was difficult for him to get men to work for him. He had however amassed 450,000 kroner and was using the money to take nine prefabricated barracks to Svalbard, together with a great deal of other equipment for the construction of a more adequate jetty, together with a power station and warehouses. When the Americans tried dealing with him, he suggested that the two companies should merge, a proposal which was unacceptable. According to Longyear, he *'then turned blue and said he guessed he would quit if we were going ahead'*.

In the end William Munroe chartered a steel-hulled steamer, *Ituna* for a monthly rate of 2,500 kroner, this including the services of a captain, and arrived off Adventfjorden on 2 June 1905. He managed his first sale of coal soon after arrival - 210 tonnes to whalers at 12 kroner per tonne, with delivery accomplished by 12 July. During the first part of the summer work progressed on lengthening the main adit, and building a mining railway and ropeway. Longyear reckoned the seams he encountered were good, and that the predecessor company from Trondhjem had been driving its exploratory adit in the wrong location.

The Arctic Coal Company was registered in 1906 in West Virginia, with a share capital of 100,000 USD. For the 1906 season there was another problem regarding ships. No spare whalers were available in Norway. In March Munroe sailed for Europe, first visiting Sheffield, where he evaluated where to buy equipment, and engaged a mine foreman and three or four English miners to work in Svalbard. William Black, the manager of the SCTC, came down from Sheffield to London to discuss amalgamation with Munroe's company. These talks were inconclusive.

In Norway, Munroe had little success in finding steamers, and the same happened in København. He did discover that mining transport equipment – railways, ropeways and suchlike, was cheaper in Europe than in America. Finally he managed to charter an iron-hulled steamer, *Primo*, which had a cargo capacity of some 850 tonnes. Departure was delayed by damage to her rudder, necessitating drydocking. There were other delays and frustrations, and the added problem of having to pay 1,000 kroner in import dues for 3.5 tonnes of explosives, delivered from Middlesbrough to Trondhjem. A team of 50 miners was taken north, accommodated in the after hold. Again, the ice was heavy, slowing progress.

On arrival, to their disappointment, they found that little work had been undertaken during the winter by the SCTC. About 500 tonnes of coal had been mined, instead of the anticipated 6,000 or more. But the coal was not subjected to any screening or washing procedures, thus lowering its quality and sale value. The company's future looked uncertain. The overwintering men had almost been without food for nearly a month. High winds made it impossible to unload the supplies for 12 days. However, during the summer more transport infrastructure was put into place – a ropeway and a surface railway. Then the miners went on strike. It was not really a strike – they wrote out a long list of demands, including more pay, and presented it to Munroe, saying that if he refused to sign it they would all quit and return to Norway on the first available steamer. Munroe was furious, they all returned to work, and gained nothing. In fact they were punished with a week of nothing but hard tack to eat. Four, possibly the ringleaders, were sacked.

Svalbard was, in some ways, the Scandinavian equivalent of the 'Wild West'. The archipelago was, administratively a No Man's Land. The lack of legislative control was becoming a problem, given incidents such as the 'strike'. Svalbard was outside British jurisdiction. The Norwegians proposed that all offences and conflicts should be settled by a Norwegian court in Hammerfest, and that managers, of whatever nationality, should have the power to exercise the same authority as they would have if appointed by the Norwegian government. One matter that concerned the mining companies was hunting. With so many tourists and hunters now visiting Svalbard, armed, and after the wildlife, such as reindeer, there was a fear that local fresh meat supplies for the resident mining population could become exhausted.

The international situation was also causing concern. The Svalbard archipelago was in an interesting location, from a geopolitical point of view. Norway was definitely keen to annexe the archipelago, which was becoming a lawless place, crime being commonplace with no laws and no officialdom to keep a check on the population's activities. Russia was also, in 1906, preparing a fleet of five vessels to visit Svalbard and northern Scandinavia during 1907, this news coming from a source in Vardø. Fears were growing that the archipelago might one day become the scene of an armed international conflict.

By late 1906 the Arctic Coal Company was negotiating a contract with NFDS for 50,000 tonnes of coal for 1907, for use by its steamers operating on coastal and local services north of Bodø. The summer total of visiting vessels at Adventfjorden that year was four regular cargo steamers and two tourist steamers (Nordenfjeldske's *Kong Harald* and Det Bergenske Dampskibsselskab's *Neptun*). Prince Albert of Monaco had bunkered *Princesse Alice I* using the SCTC's coal, and had subsequently become a shareholder in the Scottish Spitsbergen Syndicate.

Munroe sailed from Adventfjorden on 2 October 1906 on board *Ituna*, which had bunkered using the Arctic Coal Company's fuel, regarded by her engineers as being of better quality than that imported from Britain. The few tonnes which were surplus on arrival in Trondheim were donated to NSB, which tested the fuel in a stationary boiler, with impressive results – a lot of steam and very little ash. Bert Mangham was left in charge at Advent City, with the task of opening up as much of the coal seam as possible for exploitation. In readiness for the 1906/7 winter a cookhouse and messroom were built for the miners. The valley to the southwest of the mining area was then duly named Longyear Valley (Longyeardalen).

From Norway Munroe continued to Leipzig to order a ropeway from the firm of Adolf Bleichert, left his wife at Dresden for the winter, and then travelled via Sheffield to Boston. In February 1907 he returned to England, and at 22.00 on the 20th sailed from Harwich Parkeston Quay for Rotterdam on board the steamer *Berlin*, in a strong northwesterly gale. Following a very rough passage, *Berlin* was on schedule when she passed the Maas lightship, some 7.75 miles from the entrance to the channel to Hoek van Holland. On passing the buoy situated close to the northern breakwater at the entrance to the channel, she was struck by a series of large waves on her port quarter, causing her to roll heavily, and then to broach to. The manoeuvres to rectify her course resulted in her running aground on the breakwater. Impaled on her port side, she developed a severe list to starboard. An attempt was made to abandon her, but proved futile - the lifeboats were swamped. *Berlin* eventually broke in two abaft her engine

room. Of the 48 crew and 96 passengers on board, 128 lives were lost, only ten passengers - six women and four men - and five crew being rescued. Munroe was not among them. None of the company documentation he was carrying, including reports on the mining activities in Svalbard, and his plans for the future of the mines, was ever recovered, in spite of extensive searches.

Meanwhile, on 16 February Longyear and his wife sailed from New York on board the White Star liner *Cedric*, at the start of a trip to Egypt and the Holy Land. They received news of Munroe's death at Napoli, and thus changed their travel plans, travelling by rail to Rotterdam to meet Munroe's wife.

Longyear thus took personal control of the mining operations. He had acquired a ship for use by the company, an Arctic whaler, *Heimdal*, built in 1872 for a Danish concern, with a hull made of oak, between two and three feet thick, braced with iron. The timbers were thoroughly soaked in whale oil, and thus well preserved. She was overhauled and refitted at Tønsberg, being renamed *William D. Munroe*. A housekeeper was also engaged in Trondheim to wash and cook for the four men in the staff house in Longyearbyen. Longyear was apprehensive over taking a woman to an all-male community, but was informed that at 45 years of age she would be 'safe'. Also on board during the voyage north was a certain Herr Baever, sent by Bleichert to supervise the construction of the first of the Arctic Coal Company's ropeways, the materials for which came out on a subsequent sailing.

Arrival off Adventfjorden was in late May, the voyage northwards having been bedevilled by incidents of drunkenness and violence among the ship's officers, crew and the 50 hired Norwegian labourers, Longyear observing in his diary,

*'The average Scandinavian seems to have no power of resistance against temptation. And they say that they have had Christianity for nearly a thousand years!'*

It was definitely a case of being 'off' Adventfjorden, thanks to the ice - all of 20 miles 'off'. Four of the future miners completed the journey on makeshift skis, and another five set out on foot the following day. In the opposite direction Mangham and the blacksmith came out to the ship with some less than encouraging news.

## The SCTC's Winter of Discontent

During the winter there had been trouble with the SCTC, for which ten English and Scottish miners had been working with around 60 Norwegians and Swedes. The abrasive style of the ex-British Army officer, who had seen recent active service in the Boer War, and who was in charge of running the mine, tended to rub the miners up the wrong way. The Swedes were particularly offended. But some consolation was near at hand. They had discovered around 14,000 bottles of beer and other liquors and had set up an informal bar, with the inevitable result that they all got drunk. The mine manger had threatened to break up an argument by toting a gun. The miners reacted by pushing him over, and would probably have killed him had there not been intervention by some of the others, who were more sober. The manager had escaped to his house, where he was virtually under siege, not daring to come out in case some of the miners tried to shoot him. There had been other fights, and machinery and equipment had been neglected and broken. The Scandinavians had threatened that when the SCTC's ship arrived in the spring, they would seize it and take all the miners back to Norway. Among them would be the manager, who would be hauled before a Norwegian court and charged with not paying wages, in spite of the fact that no work had been done.

Those Arctic Coal Company employees remaining on board *William D. Munroe*, anchored on the edge of the ice, indulged in a spot of hunting, involving seals and walruses, which were plentiful. Eventually 16 men, plus the horse, were moved over the ice by sledge to Longyearbyen. News was received that some of the men from the SCTC had crossed the fjord and removed some of the Arctic Coal Company's stakes, replacing them with their own. By way of an apology the SCTC manager loaned the Americans two of his horses and sledges. The weather continued unseasonably cold. On 31 May there was a snowstorm, and it was so cold that the steamer's whistle froze, and had to be thawed using a kerosene torch. There were now several steam whalers now in Isfjorden, all waiting for the ice to break up, so that they could reach Adventfjorden.

The arrival of the SCTC's chartered steamer soon after the ice cleared provided an opportunity for Longyear to meet some of the company's management before they went ashore. They were horrified to learn of the state of affairs, especially since their Norwegian agent had taken orders for several thousand tonnes of coal to be delivered during early summer 1907, and had chartered a ship, at a rate of 500 pounds sterling a month, for delivery purposes. There was in fact a stockpile of around 2,000 tonnes, but it was rough coal, with a quantity of rock in it, and to make it suitable for sale, given the absence of mechanised screening installations, much hand-picking would be necessary. The SCTC had so far invested around 70,000 pounds in its Advent City project, and had practically nothing to show for that investment. When the coal was eventually delivered, later that summer, it was found to be of very low quality, and that tarred the reputation of Svalbard-mined coal over the coming years, with the Arctic Coal Company's fuel also being regarded with suspicion, even though it was of much higher quality. The problem was that on the Advent City side of the fjord the coal seams were of Jurassic origin, whereas those in Longyear Valley were of Tertiary origin. As the adit at Advent City was gradually lengthened, it was discovered that the strata deep in the mountainside exhibited serious faulting.

Meanwhile, the SCTC was still trying to deal with its mutinous miners. A request had been placed with the British Embassy in Oslo for a naval vessel to be sent to Adventfjorden to court-martial the men. The ambassador refused to intervene. The Norwegian Government was not prepared to get involved, either, since Svalbard was not Norwegian territory, and the men involved were Swedes, not Norwegians. Norway would only intervene if the British Government made the necessary request, which it did not. In the end the Swedish and Norwegian miners were taken to Norway, where the only issue investigated was whether they had proper work contracts. It was concluded that since no contracts had been signed, the Swedes were not owed any wages, and moreover, they owed the SCTC for their board and lodging during winter 1906/7!

During winter 1907/8 only around 35 SCTC employees overwintered, and mining ceased in 1908. The end result was that the SCTC put its assets at Advent City up for sale, hoping to recoup some of its costs. Its prices were too high for the Arctic Coal Company. Two ships were chartered, to take most of the moveable equipment to Tromsø, where it was sold by auction. The remaining installations, although for the first few years afterwards being in the hands two hunters who acted as caretakers, were then left to rot being looted and vandalised by other hunters and fishermen. By 1912 practically everything of value had been removed from the settlement, and what remained had been wrecked, this illustrating the state of lawlessness which then prevailed in this arctic No Man's Land. The SCTC was finally wound up at a meeting on 3 October 1917. Some of the installations still survive, notably the gas engine from the power station.

In 1916 a Bergen-based company, A/S De Norske Kulfeter Spitsbergen formally took over the SCTC's mining claims, and moved most of its remaining assets, including eight of the solidly-built barracks, some 2.5 km (possibly further) southeast along the fjord to Hiorthamn, almost directly opposite Longyear City. Here mining, first tentatively initiated by the SCTC between 1904 and 1908, was revived in response to the national fuel crisis created by the First World War, and it appears that the company was optimistic, given the scale of its investment. In 1917 and 1918 a 4.4 km 600 mm gauge railway was laid to the foot of a ropeway linking the shoreline with the mine adit, Sneheim, 582 m above sea level. The ropeway terminus buildings also survive. Production continued until the brief postwar economic boom ended in 1921, the company then going bankrupt. There was a brief revival of mining activities in 1924/5. In 1937 the Bergen-based shipowner Jakob Kjøde founded Norske Kulfelter A/S, renamed Hiorthamn Moskushamn (on account of the presence there of musk oxen) and then between 1938 and 1940 revived the mine, prompted by growing fears of war and a consequent fuel crisis in Norway. In winter 1939/40 73 miners overwintered in Moskushamn - which has since reverted to its original name. According to some sources there were subsequently some attempts at experimental mining until 1960, and there are substantial archaeological remains, including the building which accommodated the lower terminus of the ropeway, and rails scattered along the shoreline. This leads to the tentative conjecture that the railway ran from the ropeway terminus to the quay at Arctic City.

## The Arctic Coal Company's Transport Systems

During winter 1906/7 the Arctic Coal Company's mining team, supervised by Mangham, in addition to killing 80 deer for food supplies for the coming year, had prepared the first mine adit (Gruve 1a). This was situated roughly 1.2 km from the quay, at an altitude of about 230 m, and had a main entrance 12 feet wide and seven feet high, the gallery penetrating the mountainside for a considerable distance, with several cross-galleries. At the mouth of the adit there was a huge wooden hopper, into which freshly extracted coal was tipped. These hoppers were characteristic of most of the mountainside coal mines in Svalbard, the objective being to stop the coal becoming frozen and thus difficult to move. Below the hopper a gravity-worked inclined plane was envisaged. This would be used for moving pit-props, machinery and men over the precipitous scree slope to the adit. Coal, however, would be tipped into the tubs of a ropeway, which of course was unsuitable for the transport of people, machinery or other large pieces of equipment. The ropeway would therefore be supplemented by a conventional surface railway, running parallel to the ropeway, to another stockpile adjacent to the quay. Construction of the surface transport system could only take place during the summer months, was dependent on supplies being sent from manufacturers in Europe and the USA, and thus took a couple of years to complete. As regards the quality of the fuel mined, it was used for bunkering *William D. Munroe* before her next voyage south. During the crossing her chief engineer reckoned that it was at least 16% more efficient than the English coal he had been supplied with in Norway for the northbound voyage.

The slopes of Longyeardalen have been intensively investigated and mapped in recent years by industrial archaeology research teams, who have compared it with the relatively few photos taken by employees of the Arctic Coal Company at that time. As in the case of most other mining transport systems, the exact configurations of the surface networks changed somewhat over the years, so an exact record of what existed is almost impossible to reconstruct.

Much of our documentary evidence comes from photos taken during the first decade of the 20th century by John Longyear, and by the Norwegian professional photographer Anders Beer Wise, who accompanied the 1909 cruise made by Nordenfjeldske's *Kong Harald* and Bergenske's *Neptun*.

The first ropeway from below Gruve 1a, high up on the mountainside, and descending towards the jetty, was 1.2 km long. Equipped with 15 tubs, and commissioned in 1907, it had a transport capacity of around 100 tonnes per hour. At its lower end there was a stockpile, from which coal was moved, again in tubs and using gravity, via a four-track railway out onto the quay.

The railway from Gruve 1a followed the western side of the valley floor, through the mining settlement. Like the inclined plane, it carried passengers - miners going on and off shift. There was also a zig-zag path which descended from the adit to the valley floor. It is reckoned that this original railway was of 600 mm (two feet) gauge. It was later replaced, possibly around 1910, by a line of 914 mm, on a slightly different route, and rather more substantially engineered.

During 1907 VDS's former hotel at Hotellneset was used by Longyear and the other company managers for accommodation, It was not that convenient, being around two miles from the quay in Advent Bay. A steam launch was used for 'commuting' purposes. However, the management decided to move the building to the mining village, to shorten their 'commute'. Photographs suggest that the 600 mm gauge railway ran to the east of the hotel, while the 914 mm gauge track ran on its west side. Trains of mine tubs were horse-drawn.

The inclined plane, as steep as 45°, was built on wooden trestles, about five feet above the surface, to ensure that the rails were kept clear of snow. Here wagons carrying payloads or miners were moved up and down using an electrically-powered winder.

The usefulness of the rail network as a passenger transport system was invaluable. Under Norwegian law, the mining company had to pay its employees from the time when they left their houses until the time when they returned home. In that way a three-minute journey by rail replaced between 45 and 60 minutes spent on foot.

During 1908 Longyear took on Frederick Burrell as general manager, to replace Munroe. Burrell was a graduate of the Michigan College of Mines, and was fully experienced. He focused on the completion of the ropeway,

Miners ride the trolley on the inclined plane descending from Gruve 1a, in Longyeardalen.

*Svalbard Museum via Wikimedia Commons*

and brought Gruve 1a into full production. However, after two years in Svalbard he resigned, saying that he was spending too long away from his wife and family. His replacement in 1910 was John Gibson, from Pennsylvania.

Over these two years Longyear City expanded considerably. A mess hall was provided for the miners, various storerooms were built, together with a blacksmith's shop. The coal-fired power station was completed, and the transport infrastructure improved. In Gruve 1a electric lighting was installed, and the miners were supplied with coal cutting machinery. By the end of 1910 there were close on 200 buildings in the mining settlement, including three houses for use by families. In autumn 1910 Gibson addressed the question of establishing a wireless telegraph link between Svalbard and Norway, submitting an application for a concession to Telegrafvæsenet, the Norwegian Telegraph Corporation. An agreement was reached whereby Telegrafvæsenet would build a wireless telegraph station at Finneset in Grønfjorden, the Storting sanctioning this project on 3 May 1911, at a cost of 390,000 kroner. It was regarded by the Storting as an important strategic step, strengthening Norway's claim to sovereignty of the archipelago. The corresponding station in Norway was on Ingøy, near Hammerfest, the two establishments being known as Spitsbergen Radio and Ingøy Radio, respectively. Although the Finneset station was completed on 23 September 1911, the first message was not transmitted until 24 November that year. During 1912 the Arctic Coal Company built an overland wireless telegraph link from Finneset to Longyear City.

However, Gibson had more urgent problems close at hand to deal with in 1911. On one occasion he was confronted while handling a miners' strike, and was physically attacked. That prompted him to resign, being replaced in summer 1911 by Scott Turner, a relative of Longyear, and a graduate of Michigan College of Mines. The industrial unrest among the workforce, which now numbered around 120, continued during 1912. That year Gruve 2a, an adit on the opposite side of Longyear valley, was opened up, but it seems that no mining took place there at that time.

## Store Norske Takes Over

At about this time the Svalbard sovereignty issue was growing in urgency, fuelled by the growing success of the Arctic Coal Company, with a number of international conferences involving those countries who wanted a slice of the icy cake, for either strategic or resource exploitation reasons - the USA, Norway, Sweden, Russia, Germany, France, Denmark and Britain being the principal contenders. Then, in 1914 the start of the First World War put an end to formal negotiating.

Longyear City provided accommodation for 245 people, mostly miners and engineers, during the winter of 1913/14. Between 1907 and 1915 Gruve 1a yielded 173,000 tonnes of coal. Longyear did whatever he could to avoid an arbitrary take-over by the Norwegian Government, which feared for its coal imports from Britain as U-boat activity in the North Sea increased. On 1 May 1915 Turner boarded *Lusitania* on her final crossing (voyage 202) to Britain... When she was torpedoed off the Irish coast on 7 May Turner lost a number of important company documents, but he was one of the 763 survivors. Ice conditions off Svalbard during summer 1915 were very difficult, resulting in few

sailings being possible, and coal output correspondingly low. The Arctic Coal Company had no option but to suspend mining activities for winter 1916/6, with only a caretaker presence on site. By then Longyear City consisted of around 25 buildings, scattered on both sides of the railway.

Negotiations began concerning the sale of the Arctic Coal Company's mining rights and assets. Other embryo mining concerns in the district were also looking for ways to move out. In September 1916 the Arctic Coal Company sold its installations to a group of Norwegian entrepreneurs, who then on 30 November that year founded the Store Norske Spitsbergen Kulkompani A/S (Store Norske). This new company also assumed mining rights from the other local concerns. John Longyear remained a shareholder in Store Norske until his death in 1922. Longyear City was duly renamed Longyearbyen.

A substantial expansion of mining activities then began, in an endeavour to meet the increased domestic demand resulting from Norway's inability to import British coal during the First World War. There were plans to expand annual production from 50,000 tonnes to around 200,000 tonnes. It was decided to build a new quay and prepare a coal stockpile at Hotellneset. In 1917 Gruve 1a, now also known colloquially as Amerikanergruva, yielded 33,276 tonnes of coal, this falling to 19,698 tonnes in 1918 and then rising to 50,327 tonnes in 1919. Then on the night of 3 January 1920 a coal gas explosion killed 28 miners out of the total overwintering workforce of 300. The workings were closed, and the mine only yielded 20,711 tonnes that year.

The Treaty recognising the sovereignty of Norway over the Archipelago of Spitsbergen (Spitsbergen Treaty) was signed in Paris on 9 February 1920, during the Versailles negotiations which followed the end of the First World War. Norwegian sovereignty was, however, limited. Taxation was allowed, but only to the extent needed to support the archipelago and its governing body (taxes are lower in Svalbard than in Norway!) Norway was obliged to respect and conserve the Svalbard environment. Citizens and companies from all nations which signed the treaty (no fewer than 46 countries acceded during the 1920s) were allowed to become residents and exploit natural resources (including fish and minerals), while respecting Norwegian law. Svalbard was not to be used for the construction of fortifications or naval bases. Norway acceded on 8 October 1924 and on 14 August 1925 the Treaty became effective. Norway renamed the archipelago Svalbard, with Spitsbergen being reserved for the name of the largest island.

Following the closure of Gruve 1a, Store Norske then decided to concentrate on developing Gruve 2a, at an altitude of 274 m, where the coal seams were of a higher quality, and, at first sight, more easily accessible. To transport the coal to the quay a ropeway was acquired from the now abandoned Salangsverket, the copper smelter and iron ore works in Kåfjorden, near Alta in Sør-Troms, dating from the early 19th century. 5,000 tones of coal were extracted in 1920, production peaked at 207,743 tonnes in 1927, then again at 291,273 tonnes in 1940, falling to 26,342 tonnes in 1942. In 1937 production from the original adit started falling, and ceased during the following year, so a new adit, Gruve 2b, was driven, this being situated on the mountainside at an altitude of 230 m, directly above the new mining settlement of Nybyen, further up-valley.

Gruve 2a was served by a 1.5 km ropeway, equipped

The remains of Gruve No. 2, with the hillside bearing the scars of dumped spoil from the mining galleries.

The aerial ropeway at Gruve No. 3, with tubs still in place.

with 33 tubs, inaugurated in 1920. This ran to Sentralstasjon, an interchange with the ropeway from Gruve 1a, whence tubs descended to the quay. The ropeway serving Gruve 2b, commissioned in 1937, was 1.9 km long and was equipped with 20 tubs.

At the heart of the evolving ropeway (taubane) transport system was Sentralstasjon, also referred to as Taubanesentralen. This was a basic 'traffic control centre' and 'marshalling yard', and was developed from 1921 onwards, this being necessary when a new cableway was required to link the ones from Gruve 1a and Gruve 2a with the new quay facilities at Hotellneset, where a conveyor belt was used for loading ships. Each of the tubs carried 700 kg of coal, and the mines were equipped with hopper loading facilities which enabled three tubs to be filled every minute. At the Sentralstasjon the operator decided which tubs from which mines were to be held back, and which were to be directed onto the final stretch of ropeway, which descended to the stockpile near the quay. The tubs were suspended at roof level, and the ground area housed workshop facilities for the repair and maintenance of cables and tubs. Shifts were worked here, as in the mines, with six operators and six repair engineers on each shift. This was probably the hardest place to work in Svalbard, since the building had no heating, and temperatures in the mines were of course higher. An important part of the work was the lubrication of the wheels of the tubs, to ensure that they ran freely, regardless of the ambient temperature. Cableway operations had to be halted when the wind speed exceed 25 m/s, on account of the risk of loaded and empty tubs swinging and colliding. Otherwise, the ropeways continued in operation year-round, with a stoppage for maintenance purposes at the end of the year. One unique feature was the Christmas Tub, which was painted especially for the celebration and decorated with lights.

In the late 1930s, with growing fears over another international conflict and resultant domestic coal supply problems in Norway, it was decided to reopen Gruve 1, with a new adit, Gruve 1b, being driven at an altitude of 185 m, and mining starting in mid-October 1939. Here the production output is not recorded until 1946, when 18,908 tonnes of coal were extracted. Mining was disrupted by a fire between 29 October and mid-December 1948. Output peaked at 308,145 tonnes in 1949, but ceased altogether after 1950, the inner parts of the adit being used as a source of drinking water for Longyearbyen until the late 1960s.

Gruve 1b was served by a 2.4 km ropeway, equipped with 26 tubs, running to Sentralstasjon, and commissioned in 1939. A collection of buildings, including miners' barracks, existed at the foot of the inclined plane(s) descending from the adits to the start of the ropeway. This settlement was known as Sverdrupbyen, and was destroyed by fire in 1985. The exterior installations at the mine were dismantled in 1982.

Production at Gruve 2 came to an end during the night of 8/9 September 1943, when as part of Operation Zitronella (or Sizilien), during an attack launched by the heavy cruiser *Scharnhorst* on Longyeardalen, Longyearbyen (the original mining settlement) and Gruve 2 were shelled and set on fire, most of the buildings being destroyed and the conflagration in the mine not being quelled until 1962. The Taubanesentralen was partially destroyed during Operation Zitronella, and not rebuilt until 1957. At the peak of mining activities, around that date, it received coal from six mines.

Mining at Gruve 2 resumed in 1947, being interrupted by an explosion in January 1952 in which six miners were killed. Surprisingly, that was the year output peaked, at 410,158 tonnes. Between 1960 and 1964 mining was suspended on account of a fall in coal prices. It was then resumed until winter 1967/8 when the mine was deemed to be exhausted.

Gruve 3, situated at an altitude of 160 m on the mountainside overlooking the airstrip, was planned from 1928 onwards, but preparation of the workings only started in 1969, with extraction of coal beginning in spring 1971. Production peaked at 268,000 tonnes in 1981, in 1984 one miner lost his life in a fire, and in the mid-1990s output began to decline rapidly, the mine being declared worked out in November 1996. Guided tours of the adit are now offered, to satisfy the curiosity of the ever-increasing number of tourists to Svalbard.

The transport system consisted of a 2.5 km ropeway, with 41 tubs, running from the mine to Sentralstasjon. Norwegian documentation indicates that the ropeway was installed in 1921. Apparently most of the coal was moved by lorries.

Gruve 4 was situated almost adjacent to the snout of Longyearbreen, at an altitude of 160 m. Here preparations began in 1954, and production started in 1970 with 68,238 tonnes. The coal was extracted by an underground railway via galleries passing underneath the glacier connecting with Gruve 2, so there was not much surface evidence of Gruve 4, which only survived until 1971, when 16,946 tonnes were extracted. There was also a surface railway from Gruve 1b which crossed the floor of Longyeardalen, passing over the stream via the Løwøbrua. This line was still intact in 1977.

Gruve 5, also known as Olav V's Gruve, took mining beyond Longyeardalen and into Endalen, some 10 km to the east of Longyearbyen. The workings were situated at an altitude of 260 m and were served by a 7.5 km ropeway, which ran to a storage silo in Endalen, operating at a speed of 2.5 m/s and moving 125 tonnes of coal per day, its tubs spaced 48.5 m apart. In the mid-1950s a power line and telephone line were established, and by autumn 1957 a road had been built from the quay in Longyearbyen. Preparations of the adit then began. Mining began in autumn 1959, output peaking at 436,303 tonnes in 1966, and ceased in May 1972, the workings being exhausted.

Preparation of Gruve 6, situated in Adventdalen at Tridalshytta between Todalen and Bolterdalen at an altitude of 323 m, started in 1967 and mining began in 1969, the output peaking in 1971 at 367,895 tonnes, then steadily declining until 1981, when the installations were abandoned. By then it was estimated that the mine still had reserves of around 380,000 tonnes. Transport was by means of a 10 km ropeway which ran to a direction-changing installation in Endalen, which also served as a junction with the ropeway from Gruve 5, and thence to Sentralstasjon.

Between Bolterdalen and Foxdalen in Adventdalen, at an altitude of 390 m, is situated Gruve 7 or Sjuagruve, the only mine in the district to survive into the 21st century. Planning started after the Second World War, with production beginning in 1976. It was then suspended between autumn that year and autumn 1981 while the transport system - galleries and conveyor belts - was improved. However data indicate that the mine was exploited from 1971 onwards, though with very low production levels (under 18,000 tonnes per annum) until 1976, when 88,932 tonnes were

**Clockwise from above left:** The remains of the inclined plane at Gruve 4; and Gruve 5; the ropeway to Gruve 6.

*All: Bjoertvedt via Wikimedia Commons*

mined, production then peaking in 1977 at 132,464 tonnes. Very small amounts of coal (up to 1,000 tonnes) were extracted in 1979 and 1980, production then rising to 158,000 tonnes in 1982 and peaking the following year at 227,500 tonnes. Since the turn of the millennium annual production remained below the 80,000 tonnes level until 2016, when 104,197 tonnes were mined. Output in 2018 was 158,448 tonnes. Originally coal was sent down a chute to the valley floor, then moved by lorry to Gruve 6, where it was loaded onto the ropeway to Sentralstasjon. From 1987 the ropeway was abandoned on account of its operating cost and lorries were used.

Following the closure of this last ropeway Store Norske decided to preserve Sentralstasjon. Most of the pylons supporting the ropeways have also been preserved as industrial monuments, as have the hoppers at each of the mine adits.

There were of course rail networks within the mines, and visitors to Gruve 3 are able to see this for themselves. As regards the surface rail networks in the Longyeardalen district, their geography is not fully known. It appears that electric mine locomotives were first ordered in 1920 from the USA, from Jeffrey Manufacturing and General Electric. These operated off overhead wires and were thus fitted with current collection poles. Naturally, overhead wire electrification would have been impractical in the open air, on account of the severe winter climate.

Gruve 2b had an extensive subterranean rail network, around 30 km in length. On the main lines 24 kg/m and 30 kg/m rail were laid, while on secondary lines 18 kg/m was the standard. The overhead wire was energised at 250 V DC. Five locomotives are known to have worked this network, two eight-tonne and three 15-tonne machines, all supplied by General Electric.

Gruve 3 is known to have had nine 15-tonne locomotives built by Jeffry Manufacturing, one 13-tonne Siemens-built locomotive, and a type G150HVE Ruhrtaler diesel locomotive, which was formerly used at Gruve 6. Here there was a fleet of around 150 mine tubs, each weighing 1. tonnes and with a three-tonne payload capacity. Until 1986 there were also five Lee Norse rail scooters, each weighing five tonnes. The rail network here survived into the 1990s.

The gauge of the mineral lines in Adventdalen is open to some dispute. Bearing in mind the American origins of much of the rolling stock, 914 mm (three feet) seems more probable than 1,000 mm. The last mine railway closed in autumn 1996 and by 1999 the remaining locomotives had been extracted from the workings and stored in the open. The original Svalbard Museum in Longyearbyen exhibited in the open, General Electric 4wWE, one of the earlier machines. This was identified by a Russian visitor as being of 914 mm gauge.

By 1913 there were several other mining concerns active in the Isfjorden district. The Swedes were interested in the potential on the northern shore of the fjord. Another prospector was investigating the seams in the vicinity of Colesbukta, and a third had staked claims on the eastern shore of Grønfjorden, to the west of Colesbukta. Here too the Arctic Coal Company had staked claims, and sought unsuccessfully, to protect these.

The 914mm gauge General Electric 4wWE and wagons on static display at the Museum in Longyearbyen. Note the remains of the mine adit and ropeway on the mountainside.

*Author's Collection*

# Pyramiden

The mining community here, on the west shore of Billefjorden, one of the inner arms of Isfjorden, was named after the nearby 939 m high Pyramidfjellet. In January 1909 the Jernkontoret engineer Frans G. Stridsbergs of Stockholm proposed staking mining claims over parts of Svalbard in order to supply coal for the evolving Swedish iron and steel industry. The Jernkontoret (Swedish Steel Producers' Association), which had been founded in 1747 by King Fredrik I, agreed to support, with a grant of 6,000 kroner, an expedition to Svalbard by the Trafikaktiebolaget Grängesberg-Oxelösund, Sweden's largest limited-liability company, involved in forestry exploitation, mining and railway operation, the objective being to stake out claims for mining. Various areas were staked out, at Pyramiden and further south in Van Mijenfjorden. Early the following year AB Isfjorden-Bellsund was founded, with a view to starting coal mining activities. During the war a new concern, AB Spetsbergens Svenska Kolfält, took over the claims, and in 1917 started preparing the Sveagruva on the northwestern shore of Braganzavågen, an inlet on the northern side of Van Mijenflorden.

In 1910 and 1911 the Russian Government asked the geologist Vladimir Alexandrovich Rusanov to undertake an expedition to Novaya Zemlya to investigate what mineral resources existed on the islands. Then in 1912 a further expedition to Svalbard was organised, on board the ketch *Gerkules*. Following the summer of research, those on board, without consulting the authorities in St. Peterburg, set off on an attempt to navigate the Northeast Passage, sailing via the northern tip of Novaya Zemlya, and never returned. The remains of *Gerkules* were found in 1937 by members of the Soviet Arctic Institute at 74° 56'N, 86° 18' E, off Kolosovykh Island in the Kolosovykh archipelago, well to the east of Novaya Zemlya.

In the early 1920s the USSR started to develop mining activities in the Kola Peninsula, over which it had established territorial rights on 9 November 1917. The area was rich in minerals - in particular silver, copper, apatite, sulphide, titanium, iron ore and nickel. But to develop the smelting industries necessary for the processing of ores would be difficult - there were no local coal strata. Such was the scale of industrial development proposed that moving coal from other mining basins within the USSR by rail would have been uneconomical, and impractical. The nearest convenient coal resources were on Svalbard, and the fuel could be moved by sea, in large quantities. During 1924 and 1925 the Russian research ship *Persei* was sent on expeditions to Svalbard to seek out suitable mining locations.

In 1926 the Anglo-Russkiy Grumant company acquired the mining rights over an area of 47.05 km² at Pyramiden from the Swedes. The following year the ownership of Pyramiden passed to the State Trust Severoles, and then on 12 July 1931 to the State Trust Arktikugol, which, under the administration of Lazar Likhterman, assumed responsibility for all Soviet mining activities on Svalbard on 7 October that year. Development of the mining site began in 1939, the creating of the mining settlement being paralleled by further geological research. The first Russian mining team overwintered in Pyramiden in 1940/41, and by summer 1941 there were 99 residents. Facilities included a diesel fuel depot, a storehouse, radio station, boiler room barracks and bathhouse. Work started on driving the first adit, nearly 500 m above sea level.

The start of the Second World War resulted in Arktikugol having to suspend mining activities - the risk of Soviet colliers being torpedoed was too great. Under the Allies' Operation Gauntlet between 25 August and 3 September 1941 the town was evacuated, the Russian mining population being taken by *Empress of Canada* to Arkhangelsk, sailing on the night of 26/27 August. As a precaution against the installations being used by German invaders, the Russians and Allies first set fire to the fuel depot, the coal stockpile, and various road vehicles.

Following the end of the conflict Russia experienced a severe coal shortage. Many of the country's mining installations west of the Urals had been destroyed by the German invaders, so getting the Svalbard mines up and running was of vital importance. In August 1945 609 Russians returned to Pyramiden to start reconstruction of the mining settlement. They established a Soviet consulate (which was transferred to Barentsburg in 1950), and an icebreaker was stationed there during the following winter, to maintain an open lead through Isfjorden to Barentsburg, some 120 km distant. Geological surveys were resumed. The resident population at Pyramiden swelled to 350 by summer 1947, though mining did not resume there until 1950.

It was not until 30 March 1956 that what was referred to as the second adit, Severnaya (Northern) was commissioned. This had a designed output of 235,000 tonnes of coal per annum, and was situated over 400 m above the fjord. 38,000 tonnes were extracted during the first year, rising to 107,000 tonnes in 1957, the population of the mining town then being 728.

The coal was lowered by what in Russian (from the Arktikugol website) translates as an 'inclined plane' from the adits on the mountainside to the north of Pyramiden to a stockpile, adjacent to a massive loading staithe on the fjord. But in the 1950 Norwegian national mining economic report the transport facility is described as several 'transportbeltene', which seems to suggest that conveyor belt technology was preferred by the Russians. The Toposvalbard website map and accompanying Norsk Polarinstitutt photos also suggest that a ropeway or conveyor ran west from the settlement up Mimerdalen, possibly to serve workings there. Unfortunately the photos lack sufficient resolution for one to see exactly what existed, though at the western end of this transport system there is definitely a conveyor descending from the small lake to the north, on the hillside.

Photos taken on the staithe do, however, show the presence of mine tubs, on 750 mm gauge rails, the standard gauge for Russian mine networks, rather than 600 mm. Within the mine, rail transport was also used, with horse traction employed during the exploratory period until 1955, when battery locomotives were acquired. Russian sources suggest that at Pyramiden there were in all around 6 km of tracks. It is believed that the battery locomotives were transferred to Barentsburg after the mines were closed.

With Pyramiden being one of the few Soviet settlements outside of the Iron Curtain, Arktikugol decided to give potential visitors a good impression. The facilities developed there during the 1960s and 1970s were of a far higher standard than those in any other Soviet mining town, and a posting to Pyramiden was a highly coveted prize among Russian miners. But only the best technicians and

A batch of mine tubs are left to rust at Pyramiden...

... whilst one of their number has a brighter future as the 'gate guardian' of the complex, now a tourist attraction.

*Both: Author's Collection*

miners were recruited. By the 1980s the resident population had topped 1,000. There was even a 'farm' with greenhouses to meet local food requirements. In 1975 35,000 kg of meat, 48,000 litres of milk, 110,000 eggs and 5,700 kg of vegetables were produced. Both at Pyramiden and Barentsburg a determined effort was made to improve coal productivity, with the introduction of modern mechanised mining and extraction techniques. Automation even spread to the transport systems. There was also a good level of fraternisation between the Store Norske and Arktikugol miners, with joint events such as ski competitions. During the 1960s the mine at Pyramiden yielded over 7 million tonnes.

By the 1980s Arktikugol's annual coal production averaged some 550,000 tonnes. But, as the 20th century drew to a close, it was evident that the coal seams were not as rich as had originally been anticipated. Russia, following the break-up of the Soviet Union, was unable to cover the cost of expanding into deep-level mining in Svalbard. Arktikugol was restructured to become a self-financing concern. Other things were starting to go wrong, too. In 1970 a fire broke out in one of the mining galleries, and the cost of containing, rather than managing to extinguish this, was steadily increasing. It is still smouldering 50 years later…

At 10.22 on 29 August 1996 a Tupolev Tu-154M owned by Vnukovo Airlines on a charter flight for Arktikugol departed from Moskva carrying 141 people, 11 crew members and 130 passengers, of whom three were children. On account of a series of navigational errors while descending to Longyearbyen airport in blustery, showery conditions, the plane crashed into Operafjellet, to the southeast of Adventfjorden. Everybody on board was killed - around 10% of Pyramiden's population.

This was the last straw for the struggling mining community. It was decided to wind down mining activities, the last coal was brought to the surface on 31 March 1998, and a sample tub filled with the fuel was left under the huge 'Pyramiden' sign near the quay. The mine was formally closed on 1 April that year. Severnaya had since 1956 yielded around 9 million tonnes of coal. Pyramiden was abandoned, save for an armed guard, who protected visitors, coming for a fairly genuine 'Soviet' experience, from wandering polar bears. Nowadays the settlement is home to eight people, who run the hotel during the summer months. Four stay on over winter to maintain the buildings and run the power generators.

## Brucebyen

Brucebyen is situated on the eastern shore of Billefjorden, directly opposite Pyramiden. This mining settlement is named after the Scottish polar explorer William Spiers Bruce (1867-1921), who had led the Scottish National Antarctic Expedition on board the research ship *Scotia* (formerly *Hekla*, built in Norway in 1872) between 1902 and 1904, during which he established a meteorological station on the white continent, and made extensive charting and oceanographic records. Sadly, unlike Shackleton and Scott he failed to write a popular account of his explorations, and has thus remained largely unknown as a high latitude explorer and researcher. He believed, correctly, that scientific pursuit was the most important reason behind his polar explorations, and that nothing else should get in the way. In 1897 he visited Franz Josef Land,

The remains of the track to the shore at Brucebyen gypsum mine.

*Smiley.toerist via Wikimedia Commons*

and in 1898 Novaya Zemlya on board the yacht *Blencathra*, owned by Major Andrew Coats, of the prosperous family of thread manufacturers. Upon his return to Tromsø, Bruce was invited by Prince Albert I of Monaco on board his yacht *Prinsesse Alice* to participate in a hydrographic survey of Svalbard, during which the prince placed him in charge of scientific observations. A further survey was made using *Prinsesse Alice* in summer 1899. Prince Albert is generally regarded as the founder of modern oceanography.

During these surveys Bruce discovered seams of coal and gypsum in Svalbard, and also reckoned that the geology of the archipelago was suitable for the formation of oil reserves. Particular attention was paid to minerals on Prins Karls Forland, of difficult access, since the west coast is exposed, and the tidal water in the fjord on the eastern side is mostly very shallow.

Bruce's discoveries prompted him to found the Scottish Spitsbergen Syndicate Ltd. (SSS) in July 1909 with a view to mineral prospecting. A detailed prospecting expedition that summer registered claims on Prins Karls Forland (four sites - Point McVitie, Richard Lagoon, Kenmore Hut and Inchcolm Hut), Barentsøya and Edgeøya, but in general the results of prospecting were disappointing. Today several of the huts remain, together with abandoned prospecting tools scattered among the investigative mineral workings. The cost of the voyage practically drained the SSS of its financial resources - 4,000 pounds sterling. Bruce made two further visits to Svalbard, in 1912 and 1914, and was then prevented from any further prospecting activities until 1919, on account of the war.

In 1919 the SSS was restructured and refinanced, and an expedition to Svalbard was organised. Here the focus was on the eastern shore of Billefjord, where 'Bruce City' or Brucebyen was established, in the hope of finding commercially viable coal measures. During the summers 1919 and 1920 substantial infrastructure was built, this including a stretch of railway, with two sets of points. A batch of mine tubs was also brought from Scotland. Four buildings were erected, though unfortunately one of these was destroyed in a fire in 2010 in an accident caused by a group of tourists. A replica was built in 2012. No quay or jetty facilities appear to have been provided. The railway is stated as having a gauge of 450 mm (18 inches) - popular in munitions factories at that time. Current remains include a stretch of the railway, with a small wooden vehicle on the tracks.

Bruce made in all nine visits to Svalbard. However, his health was failing, and he died in Edinburgh in 1921, the year after his final visit in 1920. By then the SSS must have been in financial difficulties, since there are no signs of any mining having taken place at Brucebyen. However, the syndicate had by then filed mining rights claims covering an area of 7,709 km$^2$ on the archipelago, more than any other company. Bruce then petitioned the British Government to exert sovereignty claims over Svalbard, but very little interest was shown from London. The Syndicate survived until the early 1950s, when it was formally wound up.

## Skansbukta

The horseshoe-shaped bay of Skansbukta is situated near the entrance to Billefjorden, on the northwest shore. Here, in 1919 the Portland Cementfabrikk of Dalen, Norway, investigated the possibility of mining gypsum lodes, but then abandoned the attempt. During the 1930s Bergen shipowner Jakob Kjøde made an attempt to revive the mine, and appears to have invested substantially in infrastructure, including a short stretch of railway (gauge unknown, possibly 600 mm) between the mine adit and a timber jetty. A batch of hand-propelled metal mine tubs was also acquired. However, mining probably ceased by the time that Norway was occupied by the Germans, and was never revived. The fact that all this took place relatively recently means that a good many artefacts have survived. The railway is almost completely intact, though the timber staging on the approach to the jetty has collapsed in places. Naturally, the site is now preserved, being of great industrial archaeological interest. Also of interest to visitors are the abundant communities of Boreal Jacob's Ladder (Polemonium boreale), which produce attractive blue flowers in July and early August.

## Grumantbyen

The coastal district known as Grumant is situated 20 km west of Longyearbyen and 25 km east of Barentsburg. Here, the first geological surveys were undertaken in July 1912 by the Stavanger Spitsbergen-Expeditionen 1912, which staked claims between Kapp Heer and Colesbukta. In 1915 the mining concession was obtained by A/S De Russiske Kulfelter Green Harbour, which two years later sold it to M. Lewin & Co, believed to have been based in Oslo. In 1912 a Russian prospector, Vladimir Rusanov, together with an English partner, founded a joint-stock company, Anglo-Russkiy Grumant, and investigated the coal strata further east along the coast, towards Grumant, staking claims over an area of 80 km$^2$, and extracting the first 50 tonnes of fuel. Surveys indicated that around 40 million tonnes of coal awaited exploitation.

Following the creation of the Soviet Union, the mining rights were transferred to State ownership, British and Norwegian involvement disappeared, and from 1931 the proprietor was the Severoles Trust, followed by the Arktikugol Trust. That year in July 300 miners, led by mine captain Moisej Jevzerov Evzerov, arrived at Grumant and 2,000 tonnes of coal were extracted. There was then a huge increase in mining activity, so that in 1932 production topped 20,000 tonnes. During the subsequent decade the mine yielded around 600,000 tonnes, with a peak of over 100,000 in 1939, Russian mining equipment having been imported.

Grumant is on a stretch of coast exposed to northwest winds. To facilitate the shipping of coal, it was decided to build a quay 9 km to the west, in the rather more sheltered Colesbukta (Kolesbey in Russian). The mines and quay were linked by a railway, the original gauge of which is not known. A 1.4 km tunnel was necessary immediately to the west of Grumant under Kolberget (Ugolnaya in Russian). The rest of the line was encased in a long timber shed, to protect it from landslides and avalanches. This also enabled its overhead wire electrification.

Grumant was a sitting target for Operation Zitronella in September 1943, being destroyed by bombardments from the German warships. Apparently even the railway was obliterated. Following the end of the conflict the Soviet Government and the Ministry of Coal Mining (Ministerstvom Ugolnoy Promyshlennosti) prepared a reconstruction plan. During 1947 and 1948 over 4 km of mining galleries were reopened, a 400 kW power station was built and around 6 km of mineral railway were laid. In 1949 88,800 tonnes of coal were mined. According to the Norwegian mining yearbook for 1950 reconstruction of the railway to Colesbukta, again encased in a long snowshed, was scheduled for completion in 1951. It was once again electrified. Reports indicate that trains were formed of thirty 3-tonne tubs, hauled by an electric locomotive.

During the 1950s, as mining developed, new Soviet technology was introduced, including coal cutting machinery. In 1953 production reached 143,800 tonnes. However, towards the end of the decade it became apparent that the seams were becoming more difficult to work, and therefore uneconomical. In early 1961 the Soviet Government ordered the closure of the mines at Grumant, and the last coal was mined there on 15 July 1961. Between 1931 and 1961 Grumant had yielded over 2 million tonnes of coal.

Grumant and Colesbukta lost their last residents in 1965. From the deck of *Harald Jarl* in August 1974 we got the impression of ruins, with smoke rising from one of the buildings. The railway, in its snowshed, was clearly visible - I recall wondering what exactly the long structure was. In the 1980s some Arktikugol technicians and geologists

Three views of the derelict 900mm gauge railway from the mine at Grumant to the harbour at Coles Bay (Colesbukta). In the bottom picture the remains of the overhead wire electrification are still evident.

*D. Kharitonov via Wikimedia Commons (Top), Author's Collection (Lower 2)*

returned and undertook further investigations, concluding that around 134.4 million tonnes of coal still awaited extraction. However, it was too late. Following the fragmentation of the Soviet Union Arktikugol found it necessary to reduce its presence on Svalbard for purely economic reasons.

Both Grumantbyen and Colesbukta survive as abandoned settlements. The snowshed covering the railway has rotted away and, exposed to the elements, the trackbed has been affected by subsidence and landslips. A Russian observer reckoned that the gauge of the second generation, post-war line was 900 mm, rather a curious gauge for a Russian industrial railway. The 18 kg/m rails are marked as having been produced in Russia, some in September 1950. The power station and the transhipment installations between the railway and conveyor belt on the quay were apparently destroyed in the late 1980s, on orders from the Norwegian Government.

## Barentsburg

In 1912 a Norwegian company staked out a mining claim on the eastern shore of Grønfjorden, at that time known as Green Harbour. The company then employed a watchman, Knut Emil Glad, from Finland, to keep an eye on the claim, in case anyone decided to interfere with the stakes. Glad established himself in a hut in Gladdalen, just above the town centre of present-day Barentsburg. He also brought his wife, Anna Josefine, with him. On 9 May 1913 she gave birth to a boy, Charles Emil Polar Glad, who is believed to have been the first person ever to have been born in the archipelago.

An attempt was made to start up mining in 1916, in response to the coal shortage in Norway, but the pioneers lacked the capital necessary for investment, and in 1920 sold the mining rights to a Rotterdam-based shipping company, N.V. Van der Eb & Dresselhuys' Scheepvaart Maatschappij, which towards the end of the year founded the Nederlandsche Spitsbergen Compagnie (NeSpiCo). This concern had sufficient financial backing to develop modern mining infrastructure, and in 1924 decided to name the future mining community Barentsburg after the discoverer of Svalbard in 1596, Willem Barentsz. By 1926 NeSpiCo had developed a mining settlement, complete with its own power station, a coal-fired complex with a two-cylinder engine. The mining installations were designed for an output capacity of up to 500,000 tonnes of coal annually. There was only one problem - the company now had insufficient finance to go ahead, and had to leave the infrastructure in the hands of a small number of security guards. The assets were put up for sale.

By then, the Russians were expressing an interest in Barentsburg - after all, a fully-equipped mine was a tempting proposition. However, when the sale to the Arktikugol Trust took place, in 1932, NeSpiCo only received a fraction of the sum it had invested in the project, and its shareholders were only paid around 10% of the value of their shares. NeSpiCo was duly liquidated. By the 1930s between 1,650 and 1,900 Soviet workers were employed in the country's mining activities in Svalbard. Whole families took up residence there, and Pyramiden, Grumant and Barentsburg developed into fully-equipped mining towns, with schools, shopping and sports and leisure facilities. Mine captain Mikhail Plisetskij's daughter, Maya Mikhailovna Plisetskaya (1925 to 2015), made her debut on

the stage in Barentsburg, and went on to become one of the world's greatest ballet dancers.

During Operation Gauntlet the population of Barentsburg was evacuated to Arkhangelsk by *Empress of Canada*. The Russians asked to have machinery and stores moved to Russia on board the liner, in addition to their personal effects, and this delayed departure. Canadian engineers, left ashore, set fire to coal stockpiles and oil depot, while some of the contents of the oil tanks were released into the fjord - in more ways than one, oil is a dirty business! Remaining mining equipment was destroyed or sabotaged. *Empress of Canada* eventually sailed on the night of 26/27 August, returning from Arkhangelsk to Grønfjorden during the evening of 1 September, and sailing for Britain on the 3rd with 800 Norwegians and 186 French prisoners of war who had escaped from German captivity and had been interned in Russia. A small Norwegian defence force remained at Barentsburg, armed with two three-inch guns.

Barentsburg then fell victim to Operation Zitronella. On 6 September 1943 a squadron comprised of *Tirpitz*, *Scharnhorst* and nine destroyers, *Erich Steinbrinck*, *Karl Galster*, *Hans Lody*, *Theodor Riedel*, *Z27*, *Z29*, *Z30*, *Z31*, and *Z33*, sailed north from Altenfjorden and Kåfjorden, arriving in Grønfjorden early in in the morning of 8 September. Both *Tirpitz* and *Scharnhorst* opened fire on Barentsburg, and the destroyers went inshore to disembark their landing parties. This was the only occasion on which *Tirpitz* ever used her armaments in low trajectory fire. The task force then visited the other mining installations along Isfjorden, carrying out similar attacks, and arriving back in Altenfjorden and Kåfjorden at 17.30 on 9 September.

Only one building in Barentsburg was left intact after these attacks - the miners' canteen. Following the conflict the Russians had to start again, from scratch, to rebuild the mining community, with mining being resumed in 1949. In fact most of the present-day buildings in Barentsburg date from the 1960s and 1970s. During the 1950s, in the three mining towns, there was a combined winter population of between 2,500 and 2,900 Soviet citizens. The 1960s saw the mines at Barentsburg yielding around 13 million tonnes of coal.

The main market for coal during the last decades of the Soviet era was the heavy industrial and mining district on the Kola peninsula, and thanks to this Barentsburg survived the economic difficulties of the 1990s. In 1991 482,798 tonnes of coal were shipped out from Grønfjorden, but in 2014 only 112,038 tonnes. Things were starting to go wrong, perhaps because of a lack of attention to maintenance and safety precautions. In September 1997 23 miners were killed in an underground explosion. On 17 October 2006 Norwegian mine inspectors detected a smouldering underground fire, and mining operations were suspended while the conflagration was contained. In April 2008 another fire was discovered, and this time it was necessary to flood some of the workings with seawater, destroying mining equipment. It was not until November 2010 that it was possible to start mining again. There was a further stoppage in 2013/14, this imposed by the Norwegian authorities for safety-related reasons, following two miners being killed, and a third losing his leg.

At that time Barentsburg had a population of around 420, mostly Russians and Ukrainians, compared with around 1,000 when mining activity peaked in the 1960s and 1970s. Nowadays annual coal output hovers around the 100,000 tonnes mark, but to make Barentsburg more profitable the

A glimpse of the surface network at Barentsburg - the only true 'level crossing' on Svalbard!

*Bjoertvedt via Wikimedia Commons*

town has been opened up to tourists. In 2017 the coal output was a substantial 140,000 tonnes, of which 30,000 were consumed by the local power station, and the remainder exported to Britain. The workforce was then around 150, mostly Ukrainians, out of a total population of around 370.

Arktikugol is still the owner of the abandoned installations at Pyramiden and Grumantbyen. In all, the company has ownership rights over an area of 251.1 km², and 33 concessions for exploratory research, covering a further 320.34 km². Here there were hopes of discovering oil, gas, coal and barite reserves. These hopes have been dashed, thanks to energetic transition policies - nobody nowadays would want to create huge new mining activities on Svalbard, where the environment is highly sensitive to climatic changes.

Following an initial venture into the tourism market in 2013, in 2015 Arktikugol created a new venture, GoArctica, with 18 employees dedicated to providing guided tours for visitors. A new 90-bed hotel was created, and the former laundry house was converted into The Red Bear brewery, bar and restaurant. The objective is to convey to tourists an image of modern Russia in the arctic, and not a preserved industrial community of the Soviet era. The latter is the role of Pyramiden. Even the bust of Lenin at Barentsburg may disappear, to be replaced by one of Willem Barentsz. The Lenin bust at Pyramiden will, of course, be retained.

The mines at Barentsburg are deep, more than 1,000 m below sea level, and below the permafrost layer. Tourists are able to participate in guided tours of the workings. It takes miners over an hour to descend to the level where seams are still being exploited. Norwegian health and safety regulations apply, both to mining and tourism activities - and are not always popular with the Russians. In 2017 there were 32,000 visitors to Barentsburg and Pyramiden, of whom 600 were Russians. There are now plans for reviving Grumantbyen for tourist use. As for mining, that is likely to cease by 2024, with an output of up to 120,000 tonnes per annum until then.

As regards the Barentsburg rail network, sources differ regarding the gauge used. A British (visiting) source suggests 600 mm, while a Russian source, also following a visit, reckons that 750 mm gauge is used. In 2001 it was reported that there was a 2 km surface line, and a 20 km underground network. At the 250 m level, below sea level, there were 2.5 km of lines. The battery electric and diesel locomotives used were of Ukrainian origin. A fleet of around 400 mine tubs was in use. Around 10 tonnes of coal were moved each day to the power station, and rail was used for the transport of other materials used in the mines. There were also two cable-worked inclined planes, one for miners, the other for materials. Here around 100 tubs were moved daily. Another curiosity of the surface rail network is that it runs almost entirely in a shed, even where it crosses mountainside streams. The one open section is at the only level crossing in Svalbard! This has conventional warning signs on the road, and drivers really have to pay attention, and stop before crossing, as the trains are concealed within the sheds until the very last moment when they pop out onto the road!

Loading of coal at the quay is realised using a network of conveyor belts, the loading complex having a daily throughput capacity of between 8,000 and 9,000 tonnes.

One curiosity at Barentsburg, on the shore not far from

4wBE No. 16 at Barentsburg.

4wBE No. 5 at Barentsburg. These locomotives are believed to have been built in the Ukraine, but no further information is available.

The wagon tippler in action at Barentsburg.

*All: Author's Collection*

the fuel dump, is the existence of 1,520 mm and 2,400 mm gauge tracks. The 2,400 mm gauge rails are about 80 m long, and the 1,520 mm gauge ones 60 m long, are laid on slipways, and are used for the hauling of boats ashore.

## Isfjord Radio

In autumn 1932 two Russian colliers ran aground on Kapp Linné, on the southern shore at the entrance to Isfjorden. Arktikugol protested to Norway that something should be done about safety in the district. There was also pressure from Norwegian shipowners for action to be taken, on account of the growing quantity of shipping movements. Store Norske in 1932 had moved 243,071 tonnes of coal on board 66 vessels. There were also frequent visits by cruise liners, of ever-increasing size.

On 16 May 1933 the Storting decided that a lighthouse and radio station should be built on Kapp Linné, and provided 100,000 kroner for the project. The site chosen then belonged to the mining engineer Arthur S. Lewin of Oslo, and was known as Russekeila. However, it was preferred that the State should be the proprietor, and so 68.7 km² of land were acquired, Russekeila being purchased for 15,000 kroner. Construction took place during summer 1933, and the radio station went on air on 13 September 1933. A boathouse and slipway with crane were also provided, the radio station being situated to the southeast of the lighthouse, which was at the northernmost extremity of the headland. A 300 m long railway linked the lighthouse and radio station. Here vehicles - trolleys, most likely - were hand-propelled, and were presumably used to move supplies between the buildings. This railway was abandoned in about 1960.

Isfjord Radio was destroyed during the evacuation of 3 September 1941, and was subjected to bombardment by *Tirpitz* on 8 September 1943 - the Germans were at the time uncertain whether it was operational or not. Rebuilding started in summer 1946, the new building being very similar to the earlier one, with a barracks for up to 21 workers. In 1960 the number of staff was reduced to eight. In 1976 the radio station became unmanned, being controlled remotely from the new airport near Longyearbyen. The installations have been used as a hotel since the mid-1990s.

## The Spitsbergen Mining & Exploration Syndicate

Ernest Richard Mansfield was born in London in 1862. At the age of 16 he sailed from England to Wanganui in New Zealand, where for 21 years he earned a living as a shoemaker, banjo instructor, songwriter, poet, author, journalist and mining prospector on the Hauraki and Coolgardie goldfields. He then visited Australia in 1897, and moved to Canada the following year, having heard of the Klondike gold rush. From the Yukon he moved on to West Kootenay, where he explored the Joker and Derby mining claims at the head of the southern arm of the Kaslo River. Acting as the manager of a French mining concern, he established Camp Mansfield in the Kokanee Glacier Provincial Park at an altitude of over 2,200 m. He sailed for England in August 1901, with plans to raise finance for the construction of a marble building in Nelson. He never returned to Nelson, but instead was captivated by the prospect of marble quarrying in Europe. Camp Mansfield no longer appears on any maps, but was situated near a car park on a walking trail to the Joker Lakes.

His three years in the northern USA and Canada gave Mansfield plenty of experience of mining work in cold climates, and hence he was well-prepared for ventures in Svalbard. Having settled down, temporarily as it transpired, in Goldhanger, near Maldon in rural Essex, he made the acquaintance of the local parish priest, Revd. Frederick Gardner, and Dr. John Henry Salter of Tolleshunt D'Arcy. The catalyst for Mansfield's next mining venture came at a dinner party attended by all three gentlemen, when Salter prescribed for the weary Reverend 'rest'. Sensibly in those days, when a doctor recommended 'rest' this usually meant 'travel'. From this suggestion a voyage to the increasingly popular 'Land of the Midnight Sun' was mooted . . .

The energetic Mansfield gradually translated this relatively tame proposal into a mineral prospecting expedition to Svalbard. From his experiences on the other side of the globe he believed that much of the world's mineral wealth lay at high altitudes and high latitudes. The European Arctic could well be another Klondike. The unfortunate Gardner was duly kitted out as a gold prospector, and together with Mansfield sailed north on the Orient Pacific's RMS *Ophir*, innocently hoping to enjoy a spot of hunting in the archipelago. Following the cruise, he observed,

*'I went out to (Spitsbergen) ostensibly for sport, but, finding the land during my travels there indicated so much mineral wealth in certain parts previously untrodden and unmapped, I became deeply interested in the infinite possibilities of that country.'*

Following a shore excursion, Gardner returned to the ship with samples of rock and mud collected from streams and rivers. Mansfield was fascinated, exclaiming *'Gold, or I'm a Dutchman!'* upon examining the samples. He sent three of these for analysis by the principal assayers of the Bank of England. Small quantities of gold were found in each of the samples. This prompted the arrangement of a further expedition, for summer 1905. This time Mansfield and Gardner travelled by steamer to Norway, and there hoped to join a whaler for the crossing to Svalbard. No whaler being available, they managed to secure a passage on an ageing, and possibly unseaworthy fishing boat, the crossing lasting three weeks, during which the poor Reverend suffered from blood poisoning by drinking contaminated water.

On this occasion Mansfield and Gardner focused on Adventfjorden, where they were able to meet and discuss mining activities with William Munroe, of the Arctic Coal Company. Gardner, fearing a repeat experience of the outward passage on the return to Norway, prudently sailed from Longyear City on 17 July on board the Barbarossa-class HAPAG liner *Moltke* of 1901, bound for Newcastle. He was probably also tired out, having been sent by Mansfield on several rather long treks in search of coal samples in Adventdalen. Evidently, in those days the polar bear menace was not such an ever-present threat as it is today! Mansfield stayed on at Longyear City, to learn as much as possible about coal mining in Svalbard, and staked out a claim in Adventdalen, before sailing on 29 July on board HAPAG's magnificent *Prinzessin Victoria Luise* of 1901.

On 18 May 1906 preparations for the creation of the Spitsbergen Mining & Exploration Syndicate (SMES) began, starting with the merging the various Svalbard mining claims into a single property, and the acquisition of 650 square miles of property from Gardner. The new company, whose office was at 85 Gracechurch Street in the

City of London, started life on 1 June 1906 with a nominal capital of 5,250 pounds sterling. Substantial financial backing came from Sholto Douglas, the 19th Earl of Morton. A further expedition was mounted that summer to the Bellsund and Van Mijenfjorden district, with further mining claims being registered on both shores of the fjord. A team of mining prospectors was left to over-winter there. Capital was increased to 15,350 pounds in 1907, and further expeditions took place that year and in 1908.

On 28 June 1908 Mansfield travelled by train from London to Newcastle, to join BDS's *Venus* of 1893, bound for Bergen. He then caught a Hurtigrute steamer to Tromsø, where he hired a team of 12 labourers. They sailed from Tromsø on 9 July, and arrived in Bellsund three days later. His first task was to arrange for the welcome relief of two Englishmen who had been stranded for the previous winter at a coal mine some 12 miles distant. They had not met another human being since 25 August 1907, and sailed for Tromsø on 22 July.

Mansfield planned to spend the following winter at Camp Bell. He collected firewood, and a supply of three tonnes of coal was delivered from Tromsø. It would be necessary to maintain fires both in the living accommodation and the storeroom, otherwise many of his supplies would be spoilt - bottled produce and drinks would freeze, and then burst their bottles.

Mansfield spent the winter at Camp Bell writing his first novel *Astria - the Ice Maiden*, which was duly published in 1910 by The Lonsdale Press of London and retailed at the price of one shilling. This is a partly autobiographical work, describing his visits to Svalbard up until then, and subsequently, as the winter progressed, moving into a sort of parallel world. With reference to 25 October, he wrote,

' "Good-bye" I cried to the setting sun, when a breeze caught the folds of my flag, and waved it towards the god of life, who had now gone to gladden the homes of Southern latitudes. I hauled my flag down and kissed it. I should not want it this year-that was certain! So there we were; the flag, myself, and the shanty! We shouldn't see the sun again till the 18th of next February, and then only for a few minutes, if the sky should be cloudless!'

The novel can be downloaded from the internet for those who are interested - see; http://www.churchside1.plus.com/Goldhanger-past/Astria.htm

By 1910 the SMES had mining claims extending all along the west coast, from Hornsund in the south to Kongsfjorden in the north. One objective behind staking mining claims to such large areas of land in No Man's Land Svalbard was to assert national sovereignty rights. Most of the mines and buildings that Mansfield established in Svalbard served as markers to maintain control of their claims, safeguarding them against competitors that passed through the area in search of minerals. At this time the 'battle' as such appears to have been waged by the Americans, British and Norwegians, with Swedish and Russian interests growing. The SMES was dissolved by public notice in the London Gazette in February 1911. By then, Mansfield was already onto another venture . . .

## The Northern Exploration Co. Ltd.

The Northern Exploration Co. Ltd. (NECo) was founded on 17 November 1910, by Mansfield, Gardner and Salter. The company had a nominal capital of just 100 pounds sterling, divided into 100 one-pound shares.

In summer 1906 Mansfield had travelled north to Kongsfjorden, where he explored the island of Blomstrandhalvøya. Here what he discovered was 'no less than an island of pure marble'. Mansfield was anxious not to let the two Norwegian sailors who were working for him know what his real objectives were, so he collected some loose samples of marble, rather than blasting out large quantities. These samples he planned to take with him to England for subsequent analysis. The terrain being promising, he then asked one of his English helpers to keep an eye on the activities of the two sailors, while he and his companion, Charles Mann (who accompanied him during summer 1908) staked a claims post on the summit of the island. They then sailed south across the fjord, to the area which would eventually be known as Ny Ålesund, where they investigated alluvial deposits, and reckoned they had found traces of gold. Afterwards, they continued to Camp Morton, on the northern shore of Van Mijenfjorden. On later visits to Kongsfjorden claims were also staked on two smaller islands to the east of Blomstrandhalvøya, Juttaholmen and Storholmen. Two claims were staked rather further north, on the southern shore where Krossfjorden is joined by Tinayrebukta. Named Camp Zoe (after Mansfield's daughter) and Timnayrebukta, they were the scenes of a modest amount of exploratory quarrying, and a few huts were built for the prospectors but no commercial exploitation ever took place there.

In 1909 a specialist in the marble industry and market, William George Renwick, analysed 25 samples of marble from Svalbard, ranging from types suitable not only for basic use (such as table tops and floor tiles) but also for luxury products and quality architectural work. Standard marble fetched between 6 and 12 pounds per tonne. At that time the main world markets for marble were America, Canada, Germany, Belgium, France and Britain. These countries represented an annual demand of around 700,000 tonnes. Renwick advised stockpiling marble in anticipation of future demand.

Marble quarrying started up on Blomstrandhalvøya in 1911, the quarrying settlement on the southern extremity of the island being variously known as Ny London and Piersonhamna. The natural harbour there was named after Sidney Thomas Pierson, a chartered accountant, who was a NECo shareholder. A substantial amount of quarrying equipment was disembarked on the island. Houses were built to accommodate up to 70 people, workshops and storage sheds were erected, with separate piped water supplies for domestic and industrial use. Two quarries were opened up, and a third prepared for exploitation. Steam-powered channellers and other quarrying machinery, some of it designed to be moved on rails, was assembled, having been supplied by the Sullivan Machinery Company, Ingersoll-Rand (both USA), R. Garrett & Sons (Leiston Works Suffolk), and Schram, Harker & Co. of London. This was the only instance of this type of quarrying machinery having ever been moved to Svalbard. A steam-powered mobile crane, designed for 1,435 mm gauge tracks, was supplied by Taylor & Hubbard of Leicester. It appears that the associated 'Y'-shaped rail network, between the quarries on the western shore of Piersonhamna, the workshop and the quarry to the west of the latter, was 1,435 mm gauge. However, the only traces of it nowadays are long stretches of embankment, the rails having been lifted and stacked near the storehouse. Rather curiously, there are no 1,435 mm gauge mineral tubs on the site.

here are, however, several 600 mm gauge tubs. Temporary 600 mm gauge track would have been easier to lift and move within the quarrying areas. Quarried marble was probably hoisted by crane over the cliff edge to moored ships, in the absence of jetty facilities. The few photos that exist seem to suggest that 1,435 mm gauge track was used. For further information readers are invited to explore The Goldhanger Digital Archives, which are regularly updated.

Marble quarrying activities on Blomstrandhalvøya and elsewhere in this district was a short-lived activity. Svalbard marble had one big defect. The quarried blocks crumbled when moved to warmer climes, and were thus commercially useless. Following this fiasco, in 1913 Mansfield was dismissed as the manager of NECo.

NECo continued its annual mineral prospecting expeditions to Svalbard between 1911 and 1914, reviving them in 1918. The company steadily expanded both its share capital and the area of land over which it had staked mining claims. By 1920 it had amassed 1 million pounds in share capital. The final expedition took place in 1927, and the company was liquidated in 1934, ten years after Mansfield's death.

## Camp Morton

Camp Morton, on the northern shore of Van Mijenfjorden, had initially been investigated in 1901 by the Bergen-based shipowner Christian Michelsen, who had built a large timber building, Michelsenhuset, there. The SMES staked claims there and subsequently in 1911 transferred mining rights to the NECo, which undertook sporadic mining activity, this ceasing soon after the end of the First World War.

At Camp Morton the three mine adits were situated on a very steep scree slope, two being about 150 m above sea level, and the third rather higher. There is evidence that all three adits were rail-served, fragments of track protruding from them. Coal was lowered to the shore by means of a rudimentary inclined plane, a distance of about 850 m. Fragments of rail, wooden sleepers, pulleys and three types of mine tub survive. At the lower end of the scree slope there is even a short stretch of intact railway track. Close to the shore the railway headed west, ending at a gully, above the water of the fjord. The mining settlement appears to have consisted of four houses, two of which, including the large Michelsenhus, have survived. The two which have collapsed were probably miners' barracks. There are also the remains of a portable steam winch, manufactured by the Southgate Pile Driver Co. of London, and designed for use on 1,435 mm gauge railways. It is positioned over a length of narrow gauge track (probably 600 mm), and had probably been adapted for this gauge. Nearby are remains of a vertical boiler. Evidence suggests that although exploratory mining took place here, wooden tubs being used for the transport of coal within the adits, the full potential of the site was never realised. The seams were difficult to work, and two tonnes of the fuel were the equivalent of one tonne of good Welsh coal. The small amounts of coal extracted and loaded into tubs were probably moved by gravity and manpower. Moreover, there are no remains of any jetty, a necessary facility for large-scale exportation of the fuel.

## Camp Bell

The site of Camp Bell, on the exposed northern shore of Bellsundet, which is the outer part of Van Mijenfjorden, to the west of the natural breakwater of Akseløya, is quite different to that of Camp Morton. The coastal plain here is much wider. The original coal miners' barracks, with room for around nine men, dated from 1908, and was much closer to the shore than the existing building at the site, and although there are some remains, these could well be washed away in the future during storms. There are few archaeological remains.

## Camp Smith

Across the fjord from Camp Bell is Camp Smith, situated on the shore of Recherchefjorden. Camp Smith was established by the Norwegian consul Johannes Giæver in 1904, and was then sold to the NECo, being named after one of the latter's directors. Recent industrial archaeological explorations discovered over 40 coal mine tubs, minus their wheels, at the shoreline, together with the remains of a sturdy timber jetty, or perhaps materials delivered for a jetty which was never built.

## Calypso Beach

The idyllic-sounding Calypso Beach camp was named after HMS *Calypso*, which belonged to the Royal Navy Training Squadron, and whose crew surveyed the area in 1895. In 1901 Christian Michelsen (who became the first Norwegian Prime Minister after the 1905 split with Sweden) organised an expedition to prospect for minerals on Svalbard, investigated the site and built a house there, also known as Michelsenhuset. Around the time of the First World War the site was renamed Camp Jacobsen, after a Norwegian mining prospector and former NECo employee, Birger Jacobsen, who built a hunting station there.

The NECo started developing a coal mining camp there towards the end of the First World War. Mining activity did take place, and there is even a claim stake sign from the NECo era. There is a collapsed adit, from which the rails of a narrow gauge railway emerge, and a spoil heap. Several barracks existed, the railway, now two separate tracks, passing between them, heading towards the shore, where there are the remains of a wooden winch. On the northernmost of the two tracks between the barracks is a mine tub. By 1920 a wireless telegraph station had been established, and a mast erected, but this facility never became operational, since the same year the NECo abandoned its mining attempts there. Mining activities never expanded into full production, even though the facilities built were extensive.

After NECo's assets were sold, in 1932, a Norwegian trapper, Ole Blomli, used the facilities every winter until the 1941 evacuation of Svalbard. In 1986 a group of Poles established a research station, occupied during the summer only. Calypso Beach camp was renamed Calypsobyen by the Norwegians, and is referred to as such in current documentation. Out of the eight buildings constructed by the NECo, six are still intact, with repairs undertaken in 1992, 1995, 1998 and 1999.

## Camp Violet

Situated near Ingebrigtsenbukta on the southern shore of Van Keulenfjorden, near the entrance to the latter, Camp Violet is believed to have been named by Mansfield after his mistress, who worked as a clerk at a London hotel.

Nowadays there are the remains of two buildings, one of which was a hunting station, the other, apparently, a very solidly-built house. Investigators found two half-buried mine tubs, the only indications of mining activity here.

## Camp Millar

While the SMES's stated objective was prospecting for coal strata on Svalbard, Mansfield was also fascinated by the possibility of discovering exploitable reserves of precious metals. In 1907 he sent a few samples to Edinburgh University for assaying. These were found to contain an estimated 9.3 grams of gold per tonne, or 120 grains, and were thus deemed to be worth further investigation. Subsequent samples only yielded 16 grains of gold per tonne. Mansfield then vowed to remain on Svalbard until he had found the source rocks, this prompting his overwintering in 1908/9. In 1910 Mansfield built two houses about 1 km to the east of Camp Bell and called the settlement Camp Millar. It was here that he hoped to find gold. An adit was driven 150 m from the shore. Both houses are still intact - but there appears to have been no gold.

## Sveagruva

In March 1912 Mansfield and two NECo associates went to New York to evaluate the global market for marble, taking some Svalbard samples with them. Considerable interest was shown by marble buyers in the Big Apple, and US prices were much higher than those which could be fetched in Europe. By then the tendency of blocks of Svalbard marble to crumble when moved to warmer climates had not yet been discovered. This suggests that the first shipments of large blocks, rather than small samples, from Ny-London were not made until summer 1912.

At the time of Mansfield's visit to New York the Swedish industrialist Herman Ludvig Fabian Lagercrantz was staying at the Waldorf-Astoria Hotel. He was the director of AB Isfjorden-Bellsund, which had been founded in April 1911. An agreement was reached under which the NECo sold some of its Braganzavågen claims to the Swedes, and thus began the story of the development of Svalbard's largest coal mine, Sveagruva.

The Sveagruva mining complex is situated on the northwestern shore of Braganzavågen. Here Swedish interests, then represented by AB Spetsbergens Svenska Kolfält, started preparing the mines and transport systems during and immediately after the First World War, the first coal samples from the district having been taken to Stockholm in 1910. The investment in the transport system must have been fairly substantial, and we are fortunate, thanks to the Swedish Digital Museum website in having access to an amazing collection of photos taken around 1919 or 1920, the photographer unknown, which provides a fairly complete record (with enough gaps to keep one guessing, though!), not only of the railways, ropeway and quay, but also of life within the mining community.

In these early years of exploitation, there appears to have been at least one mountainside adit, possibly more, rail-served. From the adit(s) the railway ran along the mountainside in a southwesterly direction, in the open air, until it reached a side-valley, in which there was a glacier. Here the line was encased in a wooden gallery, which crossed this valley on a low bridge. One winter the glacier was more active than had been originally suspected, and

advanced, carrying away part of this structure, including the track. Photographs also show an open-air junction with another mountainside track, the junction being formed o' small turntables, upon which a single mine tub could be rotated, to avoid the complication of pointwork. There appears to have been at least one more of these junctions possibly several, within the gallery, and one photo indicates that there were in fact two levels of gallery, only visible from the downstream side of the bridge. Unfortunately there is no cartography relating to this first period of mining activity.

Some distance to the southwest of this bridge, the gallery, or galleries, ended at the upper terminus of a double ropeway, which descended onto the coastal plain, in the vicinity of the jetty. The discharge station here had two circuits for tubs, with mechanisms for up-ending the latter, so that their contents fell into a long hopper on the southwest side of the structure , and thence into several chutes, for the filling of tubs on the tracks at the side. Also on the southwest side of the discharge station there were various tracks serving the pit-prop yard. How the pit-props were moved to the upper level of the railway and the mine adit(s) is not known - there are no photos. To the southeast of the discharge station two tracks ran out onto the jetty, at the far end of which was another discharging installation, to direct the coal into ships' holds. Photos suggest that this part of the rail network could have been worked by gravity and cable, the jetty, which was over 100 m long, being built on a descending gradient towards its outer end.

Reports indicate that the track gauge used was 600 mm. None of the photographs available show the type of motive power used. The tubs, individually or in short rakes, could have been hand-propelled, and a number of horses were kept at the mining village, though possibly for purposes other than haulage of rail vehicles. In the report entitled *The Island Railways North of Europe* on the 'International Steam Pages' website, Richard Bowen refers to the unconfirmed use of an 0-4-0WT, and the presence of four 4wPM internal combustion locomotives built by Puch-Werke of Graz. The Swedish IndustriBaneFöreningen website, with listings of locomotives by manufacturer, has no reference to these, and does not mention the three similar machines supplied by O&K listed by Bowen. According to the latter, all these locomotives were either sold by 1922 or lay derelict. That some mechanical form of motive power existed is certain, since a photo published in 2002 on the Internet showed the underframe and air reservoir of one of the O&K machines, believed to be S10, on the shoreline.

Mining continued until 1925, around 400,000 tonnes of coal being extracted in the first nine years of mining activity, most of it being sold to SJ, the Swedish state railway company, which was in this period actively pursuing an electrification strategy. Demand for coal was falling, and its price was also dropping on the international market as the mines in Europe damaged during the First World War resumed production. In winter 1917/18 54 people over-wintered at Svea, 201 in 19210/21 and 216 in 1924/25. But Svea never developed as a fully-fledged mining community, like Barentsburg or Longyearbyen. There was no school, no church, and no shop.

On 12 May 1925 a fire broke out in the mine, and all production had to be halted. The company applied for liquidation in 1926, but was revived in 1928 as Nya Svenska Stenkolsaktiebolaget Spetsbergen, with the Swedish State as the majority shareholder. However, no

The upper end of the aerial ropeway at Sveagruva.

The lower end of the same ropeway, with narrow gauge rails leading out to the quayside. The tracks at the lower level on the jetty were for incoming cargoes such as the pit props in the foreground.

*Both: Tekniska Museets Arkiv via Wikimedia Commons*

The railway leading to the mine entrance at Sveagruva.

*Tekniska Museets Arkiv via Wikimedia Commons*

further mining took place, and the company limited its activities to repairs and maintenance. On 14 March 1934 all the assets were sold to Store Norske for one million kroner.

Store Norske originally based a workforce of around 30 at Svea, and ran the mine at a loss between 1935 and 1937, concentrating mainly on developing its mining activities at Longyearbyen. In August 1944 a wandering U-boat 'razed Svea to the ground'. Following the war, Store Norske managed to restore the mining installations quickly and between 1945 and 1949 200,000 tonnes of coal were mined.

There was then a long period of mining inactivity during the 1950s and 1960s, Store Norske deciding to carry out intensive geological research. It appears that over this period the original transport systems were dismantled, the replacement system relying on road transport. A photograph from 1970 shows a timber shed located on the lower part of the mountainside to the southwest of the jetty, while the transport system that existed between the two locations was in ruins - it is difficult to tell exactly what was there. Between 1970 and 1976 between 25 and 309 people were on site, extracting 60,000 tonnes of coal.

In autumn 1975 Store Norske revealed its new plans for Svea. The objective now was to extract around one million tonnes of coal per annum, with a total workforce of 700, of whom 450 would be employed directly by Store Norske. This was over-ambitious, and in June 1980 annual production was revised downwards to just 250,000 tonnes. The inevitable then happened again - mining ceased in 1987, and the population at Svea was reduced to a team of 12 caretakers.

The next revival attempt came in 1991. It was decided to focus on the coal measures in Sentralfjellet, and to build a road and power line between Longyearbyen and Svea. It was proposed that Svea would be developed as a dormitory settlement, with miners returning home to Longyearbyen after their two-week shifts. The road project was killed off, for environmental reasons, and instead an airstrip was built, this being inaugurated on 16 February 1995, and owned and operated by Store Norske.

It was not until spring 1999 that the Storting financed the driving of an exploratory adit in Sentralfjellet (subsequently known as Svea Nord). The access road was built during the summer that year, and in the autumn boring of the adit began. 6 m thick coal seams were discovered, and commercial exploitation was deemed profitable, this being sanctioned by the Storting in December 2001. Over subsequent years output topped 3 million tonnes per annum, minuscule in global terms, but by far the greatest output obtained from any Svalbard coal mine. This meant that, unlike most of Store Norske's Svalbard mines, Svea Nord, Europe's largest underground coal mine, was actually, at times, profitable.

Soon after the turn of the millennium detailed prospecting for more coal seams began roughly 12 km to the north of Svea Nord, at Lunckefjellet, around 650 m above sea level, with a view to commercial mining starting in 2005. However, things took rather longer than anticipated, and it was not until autumn 2013 that the mine was nearly ready for exploitation. Access to Lunckefjellet involved driving for 9 km through the workings of Svea Nord, under Gruvhjelmen, and then for 3 km across the Marthabreen (glacier), the road here even having street lamps. It was envisaged to use conveyor belts within the mine, then lorries to move the coal across Marthabreen to another conveyor belt through the Svea Nord workings, and from

One of the galleries on the railway at Sveagruva is receiving some attention in this photo (note the man on the roof in the centre of the view, as well as his colleague in the entrance).
*Tekniska Museets Arkiv via Wikimedia Commons*

there lorries down the mountainside access road to Svea, and finally conveyors to the quay at Kapp Amsterdam, 15 km from Svea Nord. The new quay facilities here were built in readiness for the exploitation of Svea Nord in 1998, and can handle Panamax-size bulk carriers.

By 2013, however, the global price of coal was too low to enable profitable mining to take place, and production at Svea Nord ceased in 2015. The global climate for coal mining in general was turning hostile for reasons other than prices, and in 2016 the Storting announced that mining at both Svea Nord and Lunckefjellet would be 'frozen' for a period of up to three years, this affecting a workforce of around 45. Lunckefjellet was originally maintained in a stand-by state, just in case coal prices recovered, and the mining galleries, all on one level, are unfinished. In 2018 the Storting announced plans for investment of 141 million kroner in a massive clean-up of remaining mining operations, retaining only those artefacts which would be of interest for future tourists or industrial archaeologists. Current $CO_2$ emissions strategies mean that the outlook for a revival of Store Norske's mining activities is bleak.

In May 2018 the Store Norske board gave the go-ahead to reopen Svea Nord, with a view to the extraction of a further million tonnes of coal. The Storting was reluctant to grant permission, even though the mining would run concurrently with the clean-up programme for the mining site. Preliminary calculations indicated that extracting the remaining coal might be reasonably profitable. In early 2019 a scientific visit to Lunckefjellet resulted in the removal of around 400 kg of coal samples. Svea Nord was officially closed, for good, on 4 March 2020.

## A Few Selected References

There is a growing amount of on-line literature and research on Svalbard's industrial archaeological wealth. I have to admit that during the preparation of this text I must have visited several hundred sources! Here are a few starters...

One useful English language reference source is *Frozen Assets, British Mining, Exploration and Geopolitics on Spitsbergen, 19804 - 53*, by Frigga Kruse of the Arctic Centre of the University of Groningen. This is part of a series of publication on Dutch research in high latitude regions.

Google the name of Frigga Kruse and you will discover various other interesting research papers in English. It may be necessary to create a free account with the Academia.edu website to download them as pdfs.

Complementary is the LASHIPA 5 report of the archaeological expedition on Spitsbergen between 17 July and 17 August 2008. This covers most sites, not only the British ones, and also includes Bjørnøya. This was also compiled by the University of Groningen. English language.

The Norsk Polarinstitutt's *Cruisehåndbok for Svalbard* is an extensive website, detailing countless locations in the archipelago. Do not be put off by the word 'Cruise' - this is a very thorough academic guide to the islands, with plenty of industrial archaeological information.

The Governor of Svalbard (Sysselmannen) regularly publishes reports on activities, projects and features of the archipelago. These are usually in Norwegian, but a listing can be found at:

https://www.sysselmannen.no/publikasjoner/rapporter/

You can spend hours and hours enjoying the Norsk Polarinstitutt's Toposvalbard cartography website. This is a bit like Google Maps, but, usefully, also with contours, and there is also a real satellite image version. The resolution of the images is good, but can be frustrating for precise detail. Beware, though, of the 'railway' symbol, which appears to cover not only real railways, but also ropeways and conveyor belts! There is of course no equivalent of Google Street View (not many 'streets'...), but there are hundreds of photos that can be enjoyed, all Norsk Polarinstitutt copyrighted.

Richard Bowen's report on *The Island Railways North of Europe*, last revised in July 2001, in The International Steam Pages website is an invaluable starting-point for research, although much has happened since then.

# BJØRNØYA

One of the island's two 0-4-0T steam locomotives heads a rake of hopper wagons being loaded.

*Author's Collection*

## Why 'Bear' Island?

Situated 235 km south of the mainland of Svalbard, and 397 km north-northwest of Ingøy in Norway, Bjørnøya has the form of an inverted triangle, with a maximum north-to-south length of 20km and a width at its northern end of 15.5 km. While most of the northern part of the island consists of a low plateau, with sparse tundra vegetation, and pitted with, lakes, the southern end is mountainous, culminating in the delightfully named Miseryfjellet, altitude 536 m, and the precipitous bird nesting cliffs at Stappen, the southernmost headland. Being situated on the boundary between cold water from the Arctic and relatively warm Atlantic water, Bjørnøya suffers frequently from mists, and with only an average of 595 hours of bright sunshine annually, is the least sunny location in Europe, in spite of its location well above the Arctic Circle, at 74°31′N 19°01′E. The average July highest temperature is +6.6ºC, the average January one a relatively mild -5ºC, rain- and snowfall are rather sparse, occurring on an average 96 days each year, and the sunniest month is May (116 hours average). The polar night lasts from 8 November to 3 February and with luck, mist permitting, the midnight sun can be observed from 2 May to 11 August. In other words, Bjørnøya is a somewhat disagreeable place, but still has a certain beauty when the sun breaks through the mist.

Bjørnøya was undiscovered until the late 16th century. Then, in 1594 Willem Barentsz organised a trading expedition, in search of the fabled Northeast Passage, to open up a new, shorter route to the Far East. On the 1594 voyage the expedition got as far east as the western coast of Novaya Zemlya, where pack ice was encountered. On 9 July a polar bear attempted to scramble on board one of the three expedition ships. The crew shot it with a musket. The bullet having little effect, they decided to capture the invader and take it back to Holland. The bear, disliking this form of captivity, threw a hissy fit, and had to be killed before it turned on the crew in rage.

A further attempt was made in 1595, involving six vessels, loaded with Dutch merchandise which it was hoped to take to China for trading purposes. Again, the furthest east possible was Novaya Zemlya. Here, on one of the islands in the archipelago on 6 September several expedition members were put ashore on to investigate the local geology. What happened next was rather alarming:

*"A great lean white bear came suddenly stealing out, and caught one of (the expedition team) fast by the neck, who not knowing what it was that took him by the neck, cried out and said, 'Who is that that pulls me so by the neck?'"*

The bear, described by Barentsz as *'frightful, cruel and big'* was evidently famished, and in an endeavour to fatten itself up consumed two of the expedition members.

It was not exactly a case of third time lucky for Barentsz, who arranged a third expedition in spring 1596. The masters of the two vessels used were Jan Cornelisz Rijp and Jacob van Heemskerck, Barentsz acting as navigator.

The coal loading staithe, with a vessel alongside being loaded, and a rake of hopper wagons visible on the structure.

*Author's Collection*

Both vessels carried cargoes of Dutch trading merchandise, bound, it was hoped, for the Kingdoms of Cathay and China. They sailed from Amsterdam on 10 May taking about a month to reach the coast of northern Norway. They then headed northwest, rather than east, hoping that further north there might be a way round the ice which blocked the coastal waters east of Novaya Zemlya. However, on 5 June they first sighted drift ice, which several of the crew members first mistook for *'a flock of white swans'*. By the 6th this ice had become so thick that it was impossible to make further headway north, so course was altered to the east. At 74°30'N they sighted land, an isolated rocky island. Using the ships' boats, landings took place on the 10th and 11th, on the latter day a huge number of seagull eggs being discovered.

On the morning of 12 June a polar bear was sighted. The expedition members pursued it in the boats, hoping to capture it. However, as they approached the bear, they reckoned that she (Barentsz in his notes almost always referred to polar bears in the feminine) was too large to tackle with their bare hands. They rowed back to the ships to collect weapons, including an axe and muskets. These had little effect when they addressed the bear with them. Nevertheless, they persisted, and at long last *'cut her head asunder with an axe, wherewith she died'*. The unfortunate bear was then taken on board one of the ships and flensed. Some of the creature's flesh was cooked, but was found to be of a disagreeable taste. Barentsz wrote in his notes *'This island we called the Beare Island'*. The name stuck even though polar bears are rare visitors to Bjørnøya.

The expedition then headed east towards Novaya Zemlya, where more pack ice was encountered. By then it was too late in the year to return to Holland, so they decided to over-winter there in a purpose-built hut. Between 15 September 1596 and 12 June 1597 they had 25 visitations by polar bears, and killed five, managing to chase off the other beasts. Barentsz never returned home, dying on 20 June 1597, soon after the surviving members of the expedition, suffering from scurvy, had sailed from Novaya Zemlya, using two of the ships' boats.

## Fragile Mineral Wealth

Over the following 150 years Bjørnøya was used as a base for walrus- and seal-hunting. Harvesting of eggs also took place from the nests of the seabird colonies. In 1603 a British expedition led by Stephen Bennet discovered seams of lead on the island. In 1609 Jonas Poole, on an expedition from London for the Muscovy Company discovered seams of lead at Måkeholmen, and on the northeastern side of the island also came across coal measures.

In summer 1827 Barto von Löwenigh, the son of the textile manufacturer and mayor of Burscheid, near Aachen, arranged an expedition to Svalbard. En route they called at Hammerfest, where they were joined by the Norwegian geologist Balthasar Matthias Keilhau. They then sailed for Bjørnøya, where in the northern part of the island Keilhau discovered evidence of several coal seams. The findings during the expedition were published by both Keilhau and

Löwenigh, but only came to the attention of a wider readership following re-publication in 1847 by Leopold von Buch, a professor at Freiberg (Sachsen) University.

This prompted a further exploratory visit, by Frederick Temple Hamilton-Temple-Blackwood, 1st Marquess of Dufferin and Ava, and the author of 'Letters from High Latitudes', on board his yacht, 'Foam', to assess the value of the coal strata believed to exist in the upper strata of the sandstone formations. He was unable to land on Bjørnøya, since that year the coast of the island was surrounded by an impenetrable barrier of ice.

Between 1898 and 1900 five German expeditions were made to Bjørnøya, with a view to considering the economic potential of the island as a whaling and fishing station. Bunkering facilities would also be required there. One of these expeditions was realised in 1898 by the Deutschen Seefischerei-Vereins (DSV), using the steamer *Olga* under the command of Richard Dittmer with coal samples being collected and analysed, the results of these analyses being published in 1901. An internal final report by the DSV was published on 17 September 1898 and reckoned that neither the seams on Bjørnøya nor on Svalbard could be worked profitably. The DSV realised a second expedition in summer 1899, and a third in 1900, this being supported by Knöhr & Burchard of Hamburg.

It appears that opencast exploitation was initially considered, but the risk of excavations collapsing was reckoned to be too great. In 1900 the excavations made during the DSV expedition of 1899 had filled with water. Adits would be more suitable, though more complicated and expensive. A cableway or railway would be used to move the coal across the flat northern part of the island to a suitable loading site. Nevertheless exploitation was regarded as economically not viable.

in 1909 the Norwegian Morten Andreas Ingebrigtsen came across both the lead and coal seams, and on 7 June that year he notified the Norwegian Ministry of Foreign Affairs that he had staked a claim across the north of the island, between Sørhamna and Nordhamna.

## Crises Prompt Mining

The next efforts to exploit the coal reserves on Bjørnøya came about partly on account of Norway's coal shortages experienced as a neutral country during the First World War, and partly because of fears that the island might be occupied either by the Germans or the Russians for strategic reasons. Mining rights across the whole of the island were claimed in autumn 1915 by the recently founded Stavanger-based I/S Bjørnøens Kulkompani, which paid 10,000 kroner for the whaling station and all mining rights exercised by Ingebrigtsen. In summer 1916 work started on the construction of a miners' community, Tunheim, and mine adits were opened up, the lead mine adit being situated north of Russehamna.

A successor company, Bjørnøen A/S, was founded in Stavanger on 3 June 1918, with offices both there, and later in Tromsø. In 1918/9 87 men overwintered on Bjørnøya, and 9,125 tonnes of coal were mined. Prospects for mining on the island looked deceptively bright. The Norwegian economy enjoyed a brief economic boom following the end of the war, and the demand for coal was high. In 1918 or early 1919 the mining company ordered two 0-4-0T steam locomotives from the Swedish company Ljunggrens Gjuteri & Mekaniska Verkstad of Kristianstad..

This company was mainly a shipyard, but between 1888 and 1919 built 38 steam locomotives. The two machines for Bjørnøya were originally known as Bjørnøya 1 (works number 34) and Bjørnøya 2 (works number 35), No.1 also being referred to as 'Pelle'.

But in 1919 the demand for coal suddenly started to drop, as Norway re-established imports from Britain. The solution for the Bjørnøya mining company was to sign a contract with the state for financial support in return for the supply of 15,000 tonnes of coal. This money was used for the construction of a 1,200 m long metre gauge railway between the mining area and a massive staithe on the east coast at Austervåg, this enabling ships to moor alongside in relatively deep, but exposed water. A new adit, A-Gruve, was opened up, a new power station built, and also a telegraph station. But by autumn that year the company was once again in financial difficulties. This time the State agreed to acquire some of the installations.

In 1920 20,000 tonnes of coal were mined by a workforce which reached 200 in the summer of that year. The adit was extended further, and Tunheim grew with the construction of a mess hall, bakery, pigsty, stables for horses, and a locomotive shed. By 1925 the economic difficulties were such that the mines were closed down in the autumn, with only a skeleton maintenance staff overwintering on the island. The fears of German or Russian occupation had come to nought.

In August 1926 the lead seams at Antarcticfjellet were investigated, but no mining took place. In summer 1927 five men were active mining, but none of the ore was shipped out.

In autumn 1927 the State granted Bjørnøen A/S mining rights for lead on the island, and the following summer 101 tonnes were mined, 96 tonnes being shipped out via the loading facilities at Russehamna. In 1929 63.5 tonnes were mined, and in 1930 69 tonnes. The Commissioner of Mines in Svalbard then produced a negative report on the lead mining activities, and this resulted in the cessation of activities.

As regards transport infrastructure, the mine adit was served by a railway, probably of a narrower gauge than 1,000 mm. The track still survives in the vicinity of the adit, whose roof has collapsed. It is possible that this railway ran as far as Russehamna, and that horses were used to haul tubs loaded with the ore.

The company now had no financial resources to develop its mining activities, the mineral market conditions were not propitious, and in 1932 all shares were sold to the State at a reduced price, the company's registered address being moved to Oslo.

Rather surprisingly Bjørnøen A/S still exists today and has a share capital of 4 million kroner. It still produces annual reports, that for 2015 being available as a pdf.

In 1918 a meteorological station was built just to the west of Tunheim, subsequently being developed into a radio station. Bjørnøen A/S ran this until 1932, when the Norwegian Meteorological Institute took over responsibility. The installations were destroyed during the Second World War and a new meteorological station was built at Hertwighamna.

Today Tunheim and Austervåg are rich in industrial archaeology, including the remains of both locomotives and several steam boilers. Even the coal railway is more or less intact - in Tunheim this divided the workers' barracks from the managers' houses.

The rusted remains of one of the steam locos.

In happier times, a posed photograph of loco, train and workers at the landward end of the coal loading staithe.

A posed photo at the foot of one of the inclines.
*All: Author's Collection*

# FAROE ISLANDS

A cable worked incline from the sea to an equipment storage shed on the island of Nólsoy.

*Jens-Kjeld Jensen*

A semi-autonomous part of the Danish Commonwealth, but not part of the EU, this compact 18-isle archipelago, whose land area covers 1,395.7 km² and whose population in 2019 was 51,371, lies 430 km southwest of Iceland, 280 km northwest of Shetland and 575 km west of Norway, at 62ºN 7ºW. The islands, of volcanic origin, date from around 60 million years ago, the eruptions followed by a long period of sub-tropical climate, resulting in dense vegetation, which formed of coal seams.

So compact are the Føroyar (the 'Sheep Islands') that nowadays practically all communications are nowadays by road, the six main islands being interconnected by roads. By the 1970s the road network was expanding steadily, and bridges and tunnels were being provided between many of the islands. The era of road tunnel boring began in 1963 with the 1,450 m long Hvalbiar tunnel on Suðuroy. Nowadays there are 17 land tunnels and two sub-sea road tunnels, together with three inter-island bridges.

The Faroese tunnel-building era culminated in December 2020 with the completion of the 11.2 km undersea tunnel between the capital town, Tórshavn, on the main island, Streymoy, and Skálafjørður on Eysturoy. Another, 10.6 km long, between Gamlarætt on Streymoy and Traðardalur on Sandoy, is scheduled for completion in 2023. In November 2016 the winner of the 152 million EUR contract for the first

of these tunnels was the Swedish company NCC. The second tunnel is estimated to cost 132 million EUR, and here it was announced in mid-December 2018 that NCC was ready to proceed.  There is even a project to link Sandoy with the southernmost island in the archipelago, Suðuroy, by a 20 km undersea tunnel, thus making the 2h30 ferry crossing from Tórshavn (and the car ferry, *Smyril*) redundant.

The Faroese topography is too mountainous, and the population too small (15 000 in 1900, 31 000 in 1950, 46 000 in 2000), to support a conventional rail network. There are, however, comprehensive bus services (free within the Tórshavn municipal district), and outlying islands are linked by seven ferry routes. But railways have in the past existed, and there are even instances of a few still being used.

## Tórshavn Harbour

The old quarter of the Faroese capital is situated on Tinganes peninsula, with inlets, Eystara Vág and Vestara Vág, on either side, where the first quays were built. However these facilities were exposed to southeasterly winds, It was not until 1913 that the Danish State granted the necessary finance for construction of a proper, sheltered harbour, and work began that year. The Danish contractor Brøchner-Larsen & Agge brought in a steam locomotive and laid 1,435 mm gauge track to facilitate the movement of construction materials. The machine was built by Hanomag, works number 1,643, in 1884 and carried the inappropriate name *'Lynet'* ("Lightning'). It was previously owned by the Hads-Ning Herreders Jernbane (HHJ, or Odderbanen), between Odder and Aarhus (now parrt of the light rail line "Aarhus Letbane", and was more suitably named *Århus* (No.2). There is some debate over its identity, since Hanomag built several other similar machines for Danish private railways, and several ended up being bought by construction contractors. Its sojourn in Tórshavn could well have been brief, since work on the harbour was interrupted by the First World War and did not resume until 1921, by which time the construction contract had been re-awarded to the joint venture Fibiger & Villefranc and Kampmann, Kierulf & Saxild. Work involved the building of a 200 m long quay running southwest from Skansatagni, to the east of Estara Våg, the area behind the quay being used for landfill, to create a 3000 m² area on which warehouses were built.

At some stage a 600 mm gauge rail network was laid on the quays, serving various warehouses. No information exists on the rolling stock or if motive power was used, or whether this network was used during the 1920s construction phase of the harbour. Quite possibly handcarts were used for moving cargoes, as was the case in many Icelandic ports. Further expansion of the quays took place between 1948 and 1954, and again between 1968 and 1972. During this latter expansion phase the contractor was E. Pihl & Søn. What is known is that in 1974 the latter concern was involved in boring a sewer tunnel in Tórshavn, and laid temporary 600 mm gauge track, using a Type 12B Eimco diesel (possibly a rocker shovel), works number 5465, for haulage. Could this track have been used previously during the harbour expansion project of two years earlier?

In 1974 E. Pihl & Søn was also engaged on another sewer tunnel contract in the Faroes. Here it is stated that two 600 mm gauge locomotives should have been used. One the contractor had acquired via Spøer of Middelfart (central Denmark) from Chr. Andersen, of Randers. This machine, powered by an Alpha diesel engine, had been on sale since 1971 and had been built by Jung in 1929. The second machine was of unknown origin. Again, documentation is vague.

## Klaksvík Harbour

With a population of around 4560, Klaksvík on the island of Borðoy is the second largest settlement in the archipelago, situated on a very sheltered north-facing inlet, and also boasting the islands' largest brewery, Föroya Bjór, dating from 1888, and now offering 11 varieties of beer, some of which are quite delicious. Construction of the present harbour began in 1935, the contractors being Styrup & Prosch-Jensen of København and Kjær & Trillingsgård. The work, then costed at DKK 589 000, was scheduled to take 30 months. Both contractors possessed narrow gauge railway material and rolling stock, but it is not known whether it was ever brought to Klaksvík.

## A Railway Project?

According to the guide who accompanied passengers from Smyril Lines' *Norröna* on shore excursions in early October 2017 there was a project for a 'proper' railway between Tórshavn and communities on the west coast of Streymoy, possibly reaching the port of Vestmanna. I have been unable to find any reference to this on Google, searching in Danish or Faroese. At least one lengthy tunnel would have been necessary, especially if the route of today's No.50 main road (Kaldbaksvegur) was followed.

## Cable Railways and Cableways

Many smaller ports in the archipelago were, and some still are, equipped with slipway cable railways, mostly 600 mm gauge. The main purpose of these short, steep railways is to facilitate the haulage of small vessels clear of storm waves. However trolleys mounted on these tracks can also be usefully employed to haul freight (such as catches of fish) from the quaysides to the centres of the villages. Sources indicate that there could have been around 17 of these railways. Some have disappeared, made redundant either by the construction of modern quays with proper road access, or by the provision of cableways, which are only suitable for the transport of loads, not boats. However some quays, situated in narrow inlets, and overlooked by high cliffs, are simply inaccessible by road, yet are still safe havens for boats, and here cable railways have managed to survive. Similarly, the easiest way of supplying lighthouses in remote locations was by sea (in calm conditions), and then by cable railway and cableway up the cliffs and steeply sloping hillsides. The cable railways known to exist are at:

- Gjógv on the island of Eysturoy. This is perhaps the most well-known, given the spectacular location of the village, at the head of a narrow inlet protected by high cliffs.

The cable railway from the hamlet to the "harbour" at Gjógv.

*Author*

- Skúvoy, on the east coast of the island of the same name. This village has around 50 inhabitants and is the only settlement on this small island.
- Mykines. This is the westernmost large island in the archipelago, and access is still only by sea or helicopter. In 2012 it had a human population of just 14(!). Humans are far outnumbered by mountain hares, the Mykines house mouse – and puffins! A cable-operated guideway, dating from the early 1960s, is active on Mykines. It links the harbour with Fjørdalsgøta, the trackway which runs west along the clifftops from Mykines village, and is used for moving heavy supplies which are delivered by boat. There is no track, since the trolley is guided by the sidewalls of the structure, on which there are flights of steps, for use only by workers and operators. Visitors arriving by sea have to use a zig-zag flight of steps, roughly parallel to the guideway.

The guided cableway from the shoreline at Mykines.

*Jens-Kjeld Jensen*

- Mykines Hólmur. Just west of Mykines lies Mykines Hólmur, an islet which has a lighthouse at its western end. This lighthouse, situated at an altitude of 110 m, dates from 1909, access from Mykines village being by way of a footbridge some 40 m above the waters of Holmgjogv, the narrow strait between the holm and the main island. A new bridge was built in 1953, and the lighthouse was automated in 1970. The present footbridge dates from June 1989. The lighthouse was fully automated in 1975. Until then the small community of keepers and their families (around 25 people, including children) had to receive provisions, and a way had to be found of avoiding the trek of around 1 km on an exposed grassy ridge from Mykines village. Only a limited amount of sustenance crops could be grown (mainly potatoes and vegetables), the community had three cows, and there was no peat for heating fuel. Electricity was generated by two four-stroke petrol engines coupled to 1.5 kW generators. In 1965 an improved transport system was created. From the cluster of houses near the lighthouse it was a distance of 300 m down a grassy slope angled at between 15 and 20º to a storehouse (both buildings visible on Google Maps, though the resolution is not good). From here a very steep 'rail-way' descended to a platform, protected with railings, with a winch, some 40 m above the sea, on the south coast. The bay or 'gjógv' here could only be accessed by small vessels in calm conditions, and preferably with a northerly breeze. The route of the 'rail-way' appears as a white strip on Google Maps, and the track, winch and platform still exist, presumably for the movement of heavy equipment for the maintenance of the lighthouse.
- Nólsoy lies due east of Tórshavn, acting as a giant breakwater. It has two lighthouses, Borðan in the south, 35 m above sea level and Nólsoy on the southeast coast, 60 m above sea level, overlooking the islet of Kapilin. Both date from 1893. There is an exposed landing place for boats on the shore below Nólsoy lighthouse, and from here there is a railway ascending steeply to a storage shed, with a cableway beyond the lighthouse building. The railway is intact, though all traces of the cableway have disappeared.

Three examples of cableways are known to survive.

- Mikladalur, on Kalsoy is famous for its seal-woman statue, whereby hangs a sad tale, situated on rocks near the sea. Here, although the boathouses, situated

The cableway at Mikladalur.

*Kim Bentzen*

high above the sea, are accessed by means of a broad flight of steps over which small fishing vessels were drawn by cables, with the help of rollers, there is, parallel to these buildings, a cableway ascending the hillside, presumably for the transport of catches and supplies to the main part of the village.

- Syðradalur, at the southeastern end of Kalsoy also has, or had a cableway. Presumably these installations can be activated as and when needed, simply by the running of a cable between the pulleys on the gantries.
- Gásadalur. A remote landing place on the west coast of Vágar is accessed by a very steep trackway, Inni á Bakka. At the steepest, lowest part of this rough track, a cableway is used for raising heavy loads from the quay.

## Hydropower and Railways

The first HEP experiments in the archipelago, to obtain electricity from water, were realised in summer 1907 by a local farmer, fisherman, and politician, Ólavur á Heygum, in the Fossá river on Vestmanna. He managed to dam the river, but the costs of installing a turbine to generate electricity for the island's residents proved too much for him. Could he also have been the promotor of the railway from Tórshavn? He was instrumental behind the installation of the first telephone line in the Faroes in 1905. He was unable to obtain any public funding to develop the HEP scheme, and died in 1923. By then the first HEP plant on the islands had been running for two years. This was located at Botni on the west coast of Suðuroy. A decade later, in 1931, Klaksvik municipality built an HEP plant in Strond. In subsequent years there was an increase in the number of power stations, both mini-hydro and mini-diesel installations. However, there was no attempt to create an integrated electricity generation system for the archipelago.

Serious planning began after the Second World War, the municipalities on Streymoy, Eysturoy and Vágoy founding the municipal power company SEV (Elfelagið Streymoy-Eysturoy-Vágar) on 1 October 1946. Demand for electricity increased substantially during the 1970s, and the power generation systems on the various islands were integrated by the laying of cables on the sea bed. At that time the focus was mainly on the use of diesel generators using heavy oil, the power station at Sund, developed between 1972 and 1975, being designed to provide sufficient power for the entire archipelago if required. It was soon realised that Sund was a vulnerable mistake – the oil crises of 1973/4 and 1979 prompting refocusing on the use of hydropower. After all, the islands receive an average of 250 days of rain annually, so water is in plentiful supply!

## The Eiði 2 Project

The main project to be realised during this period was on Eysturoy, and divided into four phases, Eiði 1 to 4. The goal was to make use of all water on the island for generation of electricity. Eiði 1 was sanctioned on 2 October 1984. This involved damming Eiðisvatn (lake), whose area was increased from 0.47 km$^2$ to 1.14 km$^2$, building an HEP

The 750 mm gauge railway used for spoil removal behind the advancing Tunnel Boring Machine (TBM) on the Eiði 2 project.
*Heinrik Hommelgard*

station in Eiði, and boring collector tunnels north to Svínabotn and Norðskála. For these two tunnels, 4 km and 6.4 km long, the contractors, MT Hojgaard and J&K Petersen, acquired a Robbins 34.35 m diameter TBM in 1984. The TBM completed its work in 1987, and the power station was commissioned on 28 April that year. During the 1990s the same TBM was active again, boring three tunnels, 3.2 km, 1.2 km and 9.9 km long, bringing the total length of collectors up to 24.7 km, receiving water from 87 intakes. By then the HEP complex had two Francis-Voith turbines, each of 6.7 MW, producing 39.8 GWh per annum. The TBM was then stored under cover close to the power station for around a decade before embarking on its third task, the development of the Eiði 2 project. This involved boring 9 km of tunnel, and excavating 2.4 km of tunnel using drilling and blasting methods, to obtain water from 32 new intakes. A further 8 MW turbine was installed at the power station, to increase production by around 16.2 GWh per annum.

During the work realised in the early 1990s 750 mm gauge track was laid in the tunnels, to remove spoil. It is recorded that three locomotives were used, together with 15 tipper wagons and one staff transport wagon (so the Faroe archipelago did indeed have a passenger-carrying railway...). The locomotives were a Type DHS125W (GIA 1260) of 1985 with a 125 HP Deutz engine and a Type DHS60 (GIA 772) of 1987 with a 57 HP Deutz engine. The third machine was a Type DHD 25, (GIA 2512) of 1997. A fourth GIA machine possibly also existed, dating from 1976, acquired by the contractor in 1980, then in the 1990s returned to its manufacturer, GIA (now Atlas Copco GIA) of Grängesberg in Sweden. It was a Type DHS60 rated at 54 HP. The open-air section of trackbed of the railway is now an asphalted access road to the service tunnel. It can be seen clearly on the north side of the Tunnilsvegur við Norðskála (route No.10), which crosses Eysturoy from Oyrar church to Skálabotni (this is the easiest route to Gjógv).

## Coal Mining

The Faroese coal measures exist on Suðeroy, Mykines, Vágar and several other islets. The only seams with significant extent are those on Suðuroy. Current estimates reckon that the coal measures here cover an area of around 23 km², and the seams are about 0.75 m thick. Suðeroy coal was first investigated in 1626, but difficult conditions made commercial exploitation impossible. In 1733 an English mining company drove an adit at Oyarnafjall, between Øravík and Trongisvágur, but gave up the following year. Further mining attempts were made at Hvalba from 1780 onwards, and in 1826 the first Faroese coal was exported to Denmark. In 1901 a French company started mining to the northwest of Tvøroyri, and in 1932 another French concern developed mining installations at Rangabotni, north of Trongísvágur, being active there for the next half-century, the buying of mining concessions being encouraged by estimates that some 10 million tonnes of coal awaited exploitation on Suðuroy.

The mines were vital to the islands' economy during the Second World War, both for domestic fuel and for fuelling the domestic steam trawler fleet. In 1954 the mines on Suðuroy yielded 13,000 tonnes, some 75% of the islands' total demand that year. It is interesting that no coal-fired power stations were ever built on the islands, and no attempts were made to exploit commercially the extensive peat bogs for fuel. Denmark paid the subsidies for developing electricity production, oil was cheap in the 1950s and water was abundant, so other alternatives were explored. Moreover, it is easier to transport energy than coal!

Rókhagi mine, 3.2 km southeast of Hvalba, and to the east of Préstfjall, has a workforce of four. Visitors can visit the mine, either by asking the employees, or by contacting the tourism office in Suðuroy. This is now the only active exploitation of coal in the archipelago, small scale mining having been continuous since the 1770s. By 21st century standards mining techniques are straight out of the

Abandoned mine tubs at Rókhagi.
*Author's Collection*

museum, although dynamite is used nowadays for blasting, to supplement picks and shovels. Carbide lamps are used for lighting inside the adits, the small workforce is ageing, and the coal is pushed to the surface in tubs, on rails. When one adit is worked out, it is simply abandoned and another one driven.

Annual output from the mines at Préstfjall during the First World War was around 15,000 tonnes, with some 150 miners, working 200 days each year. The workforce rose to 300 during the Second World War. The glut of cheap oil in the 1960s almost put an end to operations, but the oil crisis of 1973/4 saw a revival in the fortunes of the mines. However the workforce dwindled to just 15 in 1984, when only 2,000 tonnes were mined, for private use. Here the adit extended 400 m into the hillside, served by what is believed to be 500 mm gauge track. 12 hand-pushed tubs were used for coal transport, the track having simple turntables instead of pointwork, a system found in Iceland ands Greenland and also used extensively in continental Europe in sawmills with small rail networks.

At Trongísvágur – Rangibotnur the 1 m thick coal seams were exploited between 1901 and 1904 by the Société Minières des Îles Feroë using adits driven into the hillside. The company then gave up its efforts, returning again in 1932 armed with a grant and a 50-year concession to extract fireclay. This did not last long, the concession being sold in 1934 to the local concern A/S Færø-Kul. The latter, between 1934 and 1939, built a harbour at Trongisvágsförður. While the mine adits were served by 600 mm gauge rail, it appears that these fed either a ropeway or funicular descending to the harbour. In 1951 Rangibotnur mine was acquired by the municipality, and fireclay quarrying was run by the Arbeidsmanna Kolavirkid. Between 1955 and 1964 the concern acquired 840 m of rails from Spøer in Middelfart in Denmark. Some of these rails could have been used to replace worn ones. Evidently some tracks existed on the hillside, as well as in the adits. It appears that the workings were abandoned in the late 1960s.

Oyrnafjall was the scene of the British attempt to start coal mining in 1733. By 1884 more interest was being shown in this location, and according to a local newspaper there were plans to build a 2.5 km railway, descending from the adit, at an altitude of 900 m, to a terminus 300 m above the sea. It is unlikely that this line was ever built. During the Second World War the mines here were very active, at least two adits surviving into the 1950s. The coal was moved by ropeway to Trongisvágur, whence it descended via the other ropeway to the harbour. Mining continued at least until 1968.

## Military Railways

Following the German occupation of Norway and Denmark in early 1940, on 9 April that year under Operation Valentine, Britain occupied the Faroe archipelago, to pre-empt a German take-over of this strategic position in the middle of the North Atlantic. The invasion achieved its objective, the islands only occasionally being subjected to air raids, although drifting sea mines were a problem for local fishing boats.

One of the main infrastructure developments during the occupation was the construction of Vágur airport on the island of the same name, around 11,000 troops being based here. There are reports in 1943 that track, acquired by the British military in 1941, was sent to Sandavágur, some 2 km east from the airfield. The materials consisted of 219 m of track panels, 15 loose sleepers, two sets of points, four wagons, a platform wagon and a turntable. Exactly what this was for is not known. Could there have been a railway between Sandavágur quay and the airport? Some of the material was resold in 1945 for re-use at the coal mine in Kvalbø. Evidently at that time the port railway system in Tórshavn was still in existence, but could the British have dismantled it and sent it to Vágur? There is very little documentary evidence surviving from this period.

# ICELAND

Herring transport at Byggðasafn Vestfjarða.

*Byggðasafn Vestfjarða Collection via Helga Þórsdóttir*

Compared with the Faroes and Greenland, Iceland perhaps has the richest rail heritage, thanks to hydropower, farming and fishing resources, and the efforts of museums. Moreover, there have been projects, so far unrealised, for over a century for a national rail network.

The Republic of Iceland has an area of 103 000 km², and a resident population of 332,500, thus making it the most sparsely populated country in Europe. The capital, Reykjavík, has 118,912 inhabitants, its two southern suburbs, Kópavogur and Hafnarfjörður, having 31,719 and 26,808 respectively, while Garðabær, situated between the latter two, has 11,421, while the northern suburb of Mosfellsbær has 8,651 inhabitants and Seltjarnarnes, on a headland west of Reykjavík, has 4,322. The only other urban areas of any magnitude are Akureyri, on the north coast, 17,693 inhabitants, Akranes, on the northwest coast, 6,612, Selfoss, on the southwest coast, 6,510, and Haimaey, 4,219 inhabitants, this being one of the islands in the Vestmannaeyjar archipelago, situated off the south coast. The interior is virtually devoid of residents. In 1900 there were just 78,000 inhabitants, residing mostly in coastal settlements.

## Unrealised Railway Dreams

Had Iceland been able to develop even a basic rail network, involving two lines from Reykjavík to Akureyri and to Seyðisfjörður, the need for steamer services to and from the continent to be routed via the north coast could have been eliminated, with local steamer services being used to move cargo and passengers to and from ports between the railheads. Construction of railways in the inhospitable Icelandic terrain, would, however, have been a costly business although not physically impossible, and the likely amount of traffic generated would probably never have been sufficient to recoup the costs. Nevertheless, in the late 19th and early 20th centuries there were proposals which, had they been realised, would have probably shaped Iceland's local shipping service history in quite a different manner.

The first proposals for railways in Iceland came from Icelandic emigrants to Canada, who found that in their new home country the iron road had an important role in opening up new areas for economic development. In January 1989 an anonymous writer who referred to himself only as Íslendingafélagsmanninn ('a fellow-Icelander') published an article in the Manitoba-based magazine

*Lögberg*, with suggestions on how emigration from Iceland could be stemmed. He proposed encouraging Scottish farmers to move to Iceland to introduce their cultivation techniques and teach these to the locals. He also proposed that a railway should be built from Reykjavík to Akureyri, at the head of Eyjafjarður. The cost of this 330 km railway, together with a telegraph line, he reckoned, would work out at 30,000 CAD per mile, or 6 million CAD. The reaction from farmers in northern Iceland was not encouraging. Construction and operation would be problematic, they warned, because of the difficult terrain and the heavy snowfall.

The Winnipeg priest Jóni Bjarnasyni wrote in *Lögberg* in February 1890 that rail would bring substantial socio-economic and cultural benefits to Iceland, since the country still lacked an integrated road network, and the local steamship services were still unsatisfactory. Further correspondence in *Lögberg* appeared in subsequent years, advocating not only the construction of railways, but also the development of more frequent and regular steamship services, particularly linking Reykjavík and Scotland. There was general opinion that the proposed railway should continue from Akureyri to one of the east coast fishing ports, possibly Seyðisfjörður.

In 1894 another emigrant, Sigtryggur Jónasson, the founder of *Lögberg*, and who had worked as the emigration agent in Winnipeg for the Liverpool-based Beaver Line, which operated sailings between Liverpool, Quebec and Montréal, visited Iceland to further the railway cause in the *Alþingi*. The result was the Transport Bill of 2 August 1894. A company, Hið íslenzka Siglinga- og Járnbrautafjelag, was founded, its first directors being Sigtryggur Jónasson, Jón Þórarinsson, Jens Pálsson, Þorgrímur Gúdmúndsen, and the Englishman David Wilson. Its objectives were the establishment of both international shipping services and a railway. The Bill focused on both these objectives, the creation of the company, and the latter's financial aspects. The two envisaged railways would run from Reykjavík to Akureyri and southeast to Rángárvallarsýslu in the Gunnarsholt district. The company would have a share capital of 4 million DKK and would receive an annual subsidy from the Landssjóður Íslands (Iceland Land Fund) of 50,000 DKK (or ISK) until 1925, provided that train services were provided at least six times per week in the period from 15 April to 15 November, and during the remainder of the year as often as possible depending on weather conditions. Completion of the lines was to be within seven years, and the start of construction was to take place within three years, or else the company would lose all its rights and entitlements. Use was to be made of water resources en route for the generation of electricity, but the type of haulage envisaged was not mentioned.

According to Sigtryggur Jónasson the railway was to have a gauge of 30 inches (762 mm), and rolling stock was to consist of ten open box wagons, each with a 6-tonne payload, ten closed vans of similar size and capacity, four carriages with a total capacity of 100 passengers, and two luggage vans. Trains would be formed of rakes of up to 20 wagons, travelling at a top speed of 25 mph (40 km/h). By rail the journey from Reykjavík to Akureyri would be reduced to 15 hours, compared with nine days by road. En route, the Akureyri line would serve Þingvellir, some 40 km northeast of Reykjavík. Even in the 1890s the tourist potential of the site where the first Icelandic parliamentary gathering was held in 930 was under consideration – by train it would be a mere half-day return trip from Reykjavík.

The Railway/Shipping Bill was discussed at length in the *Alþingi*, receiving a rough ride, having numerous modifications (such as financing until 1915 instead of 1925), and was approved later in the summer of 1994 by 12 of the 22 elected representatives present in the *Nedri deild* (Lower Chamber). It was then blocked by the 12 members of the *Efri deild* (Upper Chamber), and thus foundered.

Plans for a rail network were revived by the *Alþingi* in 1905, when a Danish engineer, Thorvald Krabbe, was granted funding to investigate the feasibility of building a railway to the southwestern lowlands. In spring 1906 he visited Stockholm to evaluate operation of the electric railways there, submitting his plans in 1909. He envisaged a 93 km line from Reykjavík running east via Mosfellssveit, Mosfellssheiði and then south, following the eastern shore of Þingvallavatn to Ölfusárbrú and Selfoss, near the south coast. The possibility of a line running north from Reykjavík to Akranes and Borgarfjörður was also considered, as was an extension east from Selfoss to Rangárvöllur. The rail project would be combined with that of developing a telephone network for Iceland, and was championed by Reykjavík MP Jón Þorkelsson. However, doubts were expressed over whether the construction of a railway would in the end result in the economic developments, particularly in the agricultural sector, that its advocates claimed, and the huge construction cost, around 3.8 million DKK, was also seen as a deterrent. The question of electrification was addressed, Jón Þorkelsson reckoning that steam was more reliable in severe winter weather than electric, though the trackbed could be used for the laying of electricity cables.

In 1913 an endeavour was made to obtain foreign (Danish, mainly) finance for the railway project, which by then has reverted to the 1894 proposals. The opinion within the *Alþingi* remained sceptical. Railways were a luxury the poor rural areas of Iceland could go without, especially as poverty was one of the underlying factors behind the lack of agricultural progress. Construction of a railway would be too costly, and the scheme would not be profitable.

Moreover the private car had now made its appearance in Iceland, making it evident that other transport options existed – once the country's road network had been developed. On 20 June 1904 Consul D. Thomsen imported a secondhand car, built in 1901 at Max Cudell's factory in Aachen, and imports of Model T Fords began in 1913, these being ideally suited to the rough roads.

During 1914 and 1915 Jón Þorkelsson, who was an engineering graduate from the Engineering School in København, endeavoured to convince the *Alþingi* and members of the public that a reliable transport system was the reason why agriculture in Iceland was lagging behind fishing in terms of development. No produce could be sold to markets or consumers in winter, no supplies such as fertilisers or fuel, could be moved to farms, apart from by the coastal shipping services. In 1921 a Norwegian engineer, Sverre Möller, was engaged by the Icelandic authorities to survey the route for a railway from Reykjavík to Ölfusár and Selfoss. A thorough survey was realised in 1922/3, Möller concluding that the best route lay south from Reykjavík, across Þrengsli, then east to Selfoss. The cost was estimated at 6 million ISK. A 1927 street plan of Reykjavík shows that the proposed terminus of the railway would have been on the eastern side of the urban area, in the district known as Norðurmýri.

Plans for a railway were abandoned, definitively, in 1931. There are however reports that some trackbed construction for a railway linking Reykjavík with Hafnafjörður took place at an unknown date. Remnants of the trackbed survived into the 1990s in the vicinity of Hafnafjörður (famous for its huge, mostly unseen population of elves and dwarves), but may now have been obliterated as a result of urban expansion (or perhaps the elves and dwarves teamed up one long winter night and obliterated the earthworks...).

By 1930 there were 1,434 road vehicles registered in Iceland, and over 40,000 in 1970. Road construction went ahead apace throughout the 20th century, with the 1,332 km Þjóðvegur 1 (Ring Road) being completed in 1974. The total Vegagerðin (Icelandic Roads Administration) road network length in 2013 (latest data) was 12,898 m, of which 5,252 km were paved. In May 2016, there were 256,349 registered road vehicles, one for every 1.3 persons! Notably Iceland is now the fastest growing market in the world for electric cars. In May 2016 there were only 463 such vehicles, but by autumn 2020 out of the country's entire road vehicle fleet of 357,000 (of which 220,000 were private cars), 6,500 were true e-vehicles and 9,700 were plug-ins with hybrid engines. The first domestic air service, operated by Flugfélag Íslands using a Junkers W.33d seaplane, started up on 4 June 1928, between Akureyri and Reykjavík, but services ceased in 1931, restarting again later in the decade.

## Rail in and to Keflavik Airport

Keflavik airport was built by the occupying American forces (Iceland Base Command) in 1942. It was originally known as Svidningar Field, and later as Patterson Field, though referred to by the US forces as 'Camp Snafu'. An underground hospital was build adjacent to the airfield, and it is here where roughly laid 610 mm gauge track and tipper wagons, manufactured by Leeds-based Robert Hudson for the British War Department Light Railways, were used to remove spoil from the excavations, worked by the military using picks and shovels.

Keflavik airport, now a major hub for international civilian flights, was used by 7.25 million passengers in 2019. The most popular flights are those to and from Amsterdam, Boston, København, Frankfurt, London and New York. At least two coach companies run shuttle services between Keflavik and Reykjavík bus terminal, the journey taking about 45 minutes. They also offer pick up /drop off services at hotels in the capital. Domestic flights, and those to and from the Faroe archipelago and Greenland, use Reykjavík City Airport.

In 1980 a group of forward-looking MPs submitted a Bill in the Alþingi reasoning that with many of the world's oil reserves suffering from depletion, and the prospect of steep increases in oil prices in the near future, Iceland had to prepare herself for reduced dependence on imported fossil fuels and increased dependence on HEP. One project which would be necessary, it was argued, was a railway linking Rekjavik with Keflavik, with a branch serving Mosfellssveit. The engineer Hinrik Guðmundsson held discussions with DB in Frankfurt am Main over the feasibility and costing of the scheme, and broad proposals were made for the transition to a domestic electric road vehicle fleet.

Perhaps these proposals were still a little ahead of their time, since nothing further was done until 1995, when a feasibility study was made of the Keflavik rail link, envisaging that 40% of all airline passengers travelling to and from Reykjavík would use the trains, single fares being 700 ISK, and the service half-hourly, with a journey time of between 25 and 39 minutes, with an intermediate stop at Hafnarfjörður and the terminus in Reykjavík being situated in Mjódd. The construction cost was estimated in November 1995 at 7.309 billion ISK. The line would be operated by a workforce of 45. Freight would be carried, as well as passengers. By way of contrast, the Vegagerðinni calculated at that time that turning the Route 41 Reykjanesbraut from Reykjavík to Keflavik into a dual carriageway would cost around 2 billion ISK. Dualling was in fact carried out between 2003 and October 2008.

A more detailed railway feasibility study was published in October 2001, at which time completion was envisaged for 2010. It was then envisaged that the railway would carry around 1.421 million passengers per annum, and generate an annual revenue of 1.208 million ISK.

But 15 years on, the project is still no nearer take-off date, even though the number of foreign tourists visiting Iceland has increased substantially. In May 2016 a special development association, Fluglestin, owned jointly by Reykjavík city council, some of the municipalities in the Suðurnes district, the Keflavik-focused real estate development company Kadeco and Danish rail infrastructure contractor Per Aarsleff, was created, with managing director Runólfur Ágústsson. The project is to be developed privately, without any public financing, though foreign investment input is being sought. It was stated that single fares would be an astronomic 35 EUR or 4,000 ISK, for the 47 km run – which could result in many prospective passengers opting for the bus shuttle services and taxi-sharing. The scheme, presented to investors with the working title of 'Lava Express', is currently costed at 793 million EUR (102.5 billion ISK). The first 12 km of the line are to be in tunnel under the suburbs of the capital, the rest on the surface, following Route 41. Maximum line speed is to be 175 km/h. There is no indication of whether any suburban intermediate stations are to be provided, to help solve Reykjavík's chronic road traffic congestion problems by offering short workings, metro-style. The most optimistic target date for inauguration is now stated as 'mid-2024' - 45 years after the first proposals for the rail link were voiced.

In mid-December 2016 it was announced that a group of private investors was investigating the possibility of building the railway. 'Environmentalists' are concerned that the construction of the railway would obliterate part of the extensive lava field on Reykjanes peninsula... perhaps they should be more concerned that the same lava fields are visited by tourists driving motorised buggies. More important, would the community of 'Huldufolk' ('Hidden People' - dwarves and elves) living in the suburb of Hafnafjörður be disturbed by the issues caused by passing trains?

On 17 April 2015 an agreement was reached between all the municipalities in the Reykjavík district (Garðabær, Hafnarfjörður, Kjósarhreppur, Kópavogsbær, Mosfellsbær, Reykjavíkurborg and Seltjarnarnesbær) to create a light rail or tramway network to serve the district. The project is called City Line, and is to be developed by 2040. In 2007 private cars accounted for 87% of all journeys made within the urban area, compared with 68% in Stockholm, though in 2015 the Reykjavík figure dropped to 78%, perhaps a reflection of the recent economic crisis. At a municipal level

*Minør* on the quayside at Reykjavík.

*Manfred E. Fritsche via Wikimedia Commons*

the planning strategies involve containing the USA-style urban sprawl of recent years, with all new residential developments confined within current urban limits, and to encourage an increase in pubic transport patronage from 4% of all journeys made to 12% by 2030.

## Reykjavík Harbour

In the 19th century the only port facilities at Reykjavík consisted of a number of small jetties, owned by merchants, and adjacent to their own warehouses. Moorings were exposed to north and northwest winds. The first proposals for improvements to the harbour dated from 1854, but the high costs involved meant that the plans were continually deferred and regarded as impractical. By the end of the 19th century, thanks to the recent herring fishing 'Klondike', many of the small communities in northern and eastern Iceland had far superior berthing facilities to those of the capital city.

In summer 1906 Reykjavík city council commissioned Gabriel Smith, the harbourmaster of Oslo, to prepare a detailed proposal for a new harbour. The plan was completed in 1909 and the following year Reykjavík harbour committee submitted to the *Alþingi* a formal proposal for the works, the project being accepted by the passing of a Bill in 1911, authorising a Government grant of 400,000 DKK and a loan of up to 1.2 million DKK. Towards the end of 1911 the city council invited tenders at an international level for the project. The 1,570,700 DKK bid

by Nils Christensen Moneberg, of København, was accepted. This was a major piece of expenditure for the *Alþingi*, whose budget for expenditure on the whole of Iceland was 1,702,000 DKK in 2013. The project was also financed using foreign loans.

On 9 March 1913 the steamship *Edvard Grieg* arrived in Reykjavík carrying the project's chief engineer, N. P. Kirk, together with equipment and construction materials, and two barges to be used for landing the cargo. To move rocks and gravel for the construction of the two principal breakwaters and for landfill areas a 12 km 900 mm gauge railway was built, forming almost a circle surrounding the urban area, and serving quarries in Öskjuhlíð hill (stone) and Skólavörðuholt hill (gravel). The first train ran on 17 April 1913, the VIPs riding in the tipper wagons, so this was Iceland's very first 'passenger' train!

The trains, formed of rakes of between 17 and 27 tipper wagons, made up to 25 round trips per day between the quarries and the two evolving breakwaters linking Grandagarður and the island of Örfirisey (740 m), and between Örfiriseyjargarður and Ingólfsgarður (266 m). A workforce of between 100 and 140 was engaged on the project, using two steam cranes to load the tipper wagons and a steam digger to excavate the gravel and stones in the quarries. The first quay was ready for use in autumn 1915 and in October 1917 the project was completed, the railway infrastructure, rolling stock and surplus materials then being bought by Reykjavík city council. The line was

Fyrsta járnbrautarferð á Islandi.

The first passenger train on the harbour railway at Reykjavík.

Breakwater construction in progress at Reykjavík.

*Both: Author's Collection*

Hafnargerðin í Reykjavik

hen used subsequently only sporadically until 1927, when the wagons were sold to a company in Poland, though some sections of the track near Öskjuhlíð remained in situ until the early 1940s.

Two 0-4-0T steam locomotives, *Pionér* and *Minør*, worked the line. They were built in 1892 by Arnold Jung in Jungenthal bei Kirchen, works numbers 129 and 130. 4.9 m long and 3 m high, they weighed 13 tonnes tare and 15 tonnes in working order, were rated at 150 HP, had a wheel diameter of 780 mm, and were capable of a top speed of 50 km/h. They were first used in an industrial complex in Rostock, before being moved to København, and subsequently to Reykjavík. In 1910 both were re-boilered, *Minør*'s new boiler having Jung works number 1592 and *Pionér*'s 1591.

Both machines were involved in minor accidents in Reykjavík. *Pionér* was the victim of an early form of experimental vandalism'. The vandals afterwards asserted that they were only testing the locomotive's 'performance', since it had successfully demolished coins, and even wooden planks, placed in its path. However a metal chain across the tracks, weighted down with rocks on either side, defeated it, and it derailed. *Minør* became the victim of a stretch of track which subsided under its weight, since the sleepers there were rotten.

Both machines have survived into preservation. *Minør* was rather more unlucky, having first been used as a source of components for the cosmetic restoration of *Pionér*, and then being consigned to a dump for scrap metal until early in the new millennium, when she was 'rediscovered', rescued, and cosmetically restored. She is now plinthed on a short stretch of track near the southern end of the harbour, not far from the quay used by cruise liners, surrounded by a display of old photos of the harbour. With deference to her age, *Minør* is moved indoors during the Icelandic winter.

*Pionér* was exhibited on the quayside in 1961/2 as part of the 175th anniversary of the founding of Reykjavík as a city. She was then handed over to the Árbær Open Air Museum in the suburb of Kistuhyl, where after a decade stored outdoors she was subjected to a thorough

*Pioner*, preserved at Árbær Open Air Museum.

*Sigur Laugur*

restoration in 1972, and is now an interior exhibit.

There may have been more locomotives. N. C. Moneberg is recorded as having acquired Jung-built works number 748, dating from 1894, for port construction in 1916 and 1917, but there is documentary evidence of the machine having been in København in the latter year, and perhaps it never even left the Danish capital. Then there was sister machine, works number 749, also built in 1904, and owned by N. C. Moneberg. If it ever really went to Reykjavík, it was probably scrapped there in the 1920s.

The Árbær Open Air Museum is open daily, all day between June and August, for one hour each day for the remainder of the year at 13.00 (see http://borgarsogusafn.is/en/arbaer-open-air-museum).

## Stockfish Railways in Reykjavík

Quayside railways for the transport of fish and ice between ships, processing areas and storehouses were once quite commonplace in Iceland. Most of these short lines were operated without locomotives, using handcarts. Nevertheless, their importance as rail transport systems should not be overlooked, and during their lifetimes these lines must have handled many thousands, indeed millions of tonnes of freight! It is known that there were two short

Cod drying at Kurjusandur, Reykjavík, pre-1898. Note the railway traversing the fish.

*Sigfús Eymundsson Archive*

lines in Reykjavík, a quite lengthy one at Kirkjusandur, where in the late 1890s the cod were dried on the ground, and another at Fiskverkun, but information is sparse. Viðey, an island near Reykjavík, also had a railway linking the quay, the barrel storage area for salted cod, and a warehouse, believed to have been operational from around 1900 to 1940. Large handcarts were used for transport of the fish, and photos indicate that the quay had quite impressive trackwork, the gauge looking decidedly broader than 600 mm! Engey, an uninhabited island to the west of Viðey, had a short Faeroe-style railway linking the boat landing-place on the west coast with the few houses there, which were still inhabited at the time of the Second World War. All traces of the houses, and of the railway, have now disappeared.

## Korpúlfsstaðir Estate

The large (106 hectare) Korpúlfsstaðir estate dates back to 1234, but relatively little is known about its history until 1922, when it was bought by the Icelandic entrepreneur Thor Jensen, who planned to turn it into an industrialised dairy farm. In 1929 construction of a large building with 39 bedrooms and a dining room for 70 estate workers was completed. In 1930 a 600 mm gauge railway was built for the transport of fodder required for the herd of 300 cows, which produced some 800 000 litres of milk per annum. Four-wheel hand-pushed skips were used for transport, and there are no records of any locomotives ever being used.

In 1942 the property was acquired by Reykjavík city council, which used the main building as a storehouse, where municipal works of art were housed. On 18 January 1969 much of the building was damaged by fire, with the loss of many valuable works of art. Dairying ceased in 1970, though the railway survived until 1993. Afterwards the track was lifted, to enable the pastures to be redeveloped in 1995 as a golf course. In 1999 part of the main building was rehabilitated as a primary school, to cater for an overflow of pupils caused by the rapid population increase in the Reykjavík district. Following

Iceland's indoor railway - there are a couple of surviving stretches of track of the rail network which served the Korpúlfsstaðir farm estate, which is now an arts centre. This one appears to have served for mucking out the cattle stalls.

*Author's Collection*

closure of the school, Galleri Korpúlfsstaðir was founded on 27 May 2011. It is a base for 15 artists, who have studios in the main building, these being open to the public. There is a surviving 'T'-shaped stretch of track in one of the art galleries, incorporating one of the skips and two turntables for the latter. Galleri Korpúlfsstaðir is thus one of the two 'railway operators' currently existing in Iceland!

## Hvalfjörður - Hvítanes

During the Second World War the British and American occupying forces built a naval base at Hvítanes, which the Marines referred to as 'Valley Forge' on Hvalfjörður, to the north of Reyjavik.The Royal Navy soon established a tank farm there for oil storage purposes. A stretch of 610 mm gauge track was supplied by Robert Hudson, and here a 40 HP Simplex diesel ran. This track was still intact after the turn of the millennium.

A 1,435 mm gauge track served a jetty, and was used by two steam cranes. One of the 1,435 mm gauge wagons used here has been preserved by the local Hernámssetrinu (Occupation Centre) museum in Akranes.

## Eskifjörður

This east coast port had a railway, of unknown gauge, linking the quay with a shed used by the crews of whalers for dealing with their catches. The carts for transport of whale meat were pushed by hand. Photographic evidence dates the railway as being in existence in 1907.

## Siglufjörður

Situated to the northwest of Akureyri, Siglufjörður was a major herring fishing port between the 1920s and 1950s, the catches being salted in barrels, or used for fish meal, this destined for use as animal fodder or fertiliser. Between 1900 and the late 1960s there were at least four short stretches of 750 mm gauge railway, two on each quay, linking the fishing boat moorings with the human 'assembly lines' at the landward end of these quays where the fish were salted and barrelled. Literally millions of tonnes of herring were handled in this manner, being moved using handcarts on rails, the barrels often being double-stacked. One of the fish meal factories purchased an old steam locomotive (could this have been Jung-built 749 from Reykjavík, or a boiler donated from one of the other locomotives?) for use as a stationary boiler, which is why local residents always referred to this factory in Danish as 'lokomativet' ('the locomotive'). Visit the Herring Era Museum (http://www.sild.is/en) to find out more!

Herring, rail and shipping at Siglufjörður.

*Author's Collection*

## Ísafjörður

The Westfjords Heritage Museum (Byggðasafn Vestfjarða) in northwest Iceland holds the prize for the narrowest of rail gauges in Iceland – 460 mm, and the distinction of being the only 'open air railway operator' in the country!

The shortest public railway in Iceland, at the Byggðasafn Vestfjarða museum in Ísafjörður. The 'clock tower'-like structure was used by the manager to supervise workers.
*Byggðasafn Vestfjarða Collection via Helga Þórsdóttir*

There was an earlier railway, built by a Danish merchant, W. Sass, between 1850 and 1860, for the movement of fish to and from the stockfish (usually unsalted, dried cod) drying racks. Photographic evidence suggests that the line was quite extensive, possibly even running the length of the peninsula on which the village is situated. On one quay there were even three parallel tracks, and tipper wagons were used instead of the usual flat handcarts! Modern urban development now covers some of the areas where the cod were dried, but some vestiges of this railway survived until the late 1980s, when the museum was developed, using a complex of restored 18th century buildings. The modern railway is laid on a 'T'-shaped wooden base, and there are a couple of wooden handcarts. In addition to being a 'railway operator', the museum specialises in the restoration of old boats, and also has a collection of over 190 accordions, the oldest dating from 1830.

## Sauðárkrókur

Situated on the north coast to the west of Siglufjörður, Sauðárkrókur also enjoyed the 'herring boom' of the 1920 to 1950s. Here a double track line, probably of 600 mm gauge, existed on the quays in the 1930s. There exists a photo of King Kristján X of Denmark standing on the track during a state visit to Iceland between 18 and 27 June 1936, prior to travelling by steamer to Akureyri.

## Patreksfjörður – Geiseyri

Geiseyri, on the northern shore of Patreksfjörður in Westfjord, the district of Iceland closest to Greenland, had a railway serving the stockfish drying grounds, gauge 600 mm or perhaps less. Photographic evidence indicates that it was in use circa 1905.

## Eyjafjörður - Akureyri

In 1914 Dagvardareyri, about 1.5 km from Akureyri, at the head of the longest fjord in northern Iceland, was the home of the Oslo-based concern Øfjordens Sildeolie- & Guanofabrik. With the fertiliser industry then in its infancy, local guano was used, rather than Chilean imports. Danish newspapers of summer 1914 refer to the fact that the factory had a railway with tipper wagons. However in October 1913 there was also a report that the factory, whose construction had started in 1912, and which had started production in summer 1913 had been damaged by fire.

## Þingeyri

A slipway here is fitted with a 750 mm gauge track, and a locally-built diesel tractor was used until relatively recent times to haul trawlers out of the water for repairs.

This is only a brief review of those Icelandic ports for which I have found photographs or other documentary evidence of quayside railways. There probably were many others, especially those which experienced a boom in herring fishing and processing in the late 19th and early 20th centuries.

## Kárahnjúkar HEP

Aluminium does not occur naturally as an element. It is created by the refining of bauxite, 50% of which is mined in Guinea, Australia and Brazil, into alumina, by means of the Bayer process, which requires heating and the input of sodium hydroxide. A by-product of the Bayer process is red mud waste – two units of the latter to one unit of alumina. The alumina is then smelted into aluminium, using the Hall-Hérault process, which involves dissolving the alumina in a mixture of cryolite, and then electrolysing to result in the formation of pure aluminium. The amount of aluminium produced is proportional to the size of the electric current passing through the cells in which the electrolysis takes place. By-products are hydrogen fluoride (toxic and corrosive if not treated) and $CO_2$. To avoid the risk of the molten mixtures in the electrolysis cells solidifying, the electricity supply must be highly reliable, and the electricity production source must be located nearby.

So much for the chemistry lesson. 41% of the world's aluminium is produced in China, 9% in Russia, 5% in Australia - and 2% (780,000 tonnes in 2010) in Iceland, where there are now three aluminium smelters, Rio Tinto Alcan at Straumsvik, Norðurál (a Century Aluminium Corporation subsidiary) at Grundartangi (these smelters situated to the south and north of Reykjavík respectively), and the controversial Alcoa Fjardaal smelter, near Reyðarfjörður on the east coast. In 2010 these three establishments required 12,453 GWh – around 7% of all Iceland's power consumption, and employed 1,400 people. Alcoa built its smelter between 2004 and 2007, the contractor being Bechtel, which employed an international workforce of around 2,800, the majority of labourers being Poles, though 42 nationalities were represented. The smelter reached full capacity in April 2008, producing 940 tonnes per day with a workforce of 450. It is thus a major local source of employment.

Naturally, a reliable source of electricity was necessary for Alcoa Fjardaal. Between 1975 and 2002 there were various plans to capture the hydroelectric potential of the Jökulsá á Dal and Jökulsá í Fljótsdal rivers in the nearby municipality of Fljótsdalshérað and use this electricity for a major industrial complex. Naturally, there was much opposition, on environmental grounds – the reservoir creation would result in the flooding of areas with a diversity of plant life. There were also fears that Iceland's pristine drinking water sources might become – even slightly – contaminated by heavy metals.

The multinational, Alcoa, had its way, persuading the Alþingi and the Icelandic national power company, Landsvirkjun, of the viability of the 1.3 billion USD scheme, which was funded by Landsvirkjun. The main contractor was the Italian company Impreglio, with sub-contractors DSD-NOWLL of Würzburg and ATB Riva Calzoni of Italy. The workforce of around 1,200 was also international, 45 nationalities being represented, 41% from China, 28% from Portugal, and only 88 Icelandic nationals (Iceland's unemployment rate was then around only 2%). At the work camps shuttle buses were used to move workers to and from the work sites and adits accessing the tunnels, only management being allowed to use private cars.

Five massive dams were built, three on the Jökulsá í Fljótsdal river and two on the Jökulsá á Dal, both of which drain the northeastern end of the Vatnajökull glacier. All water used in electricity production at the Fljótsdalur power station is eventually discharged into the Jökulsá í Fljótsdal river. The Kárahnjúkastífla dam, on the latter watercourse, is 193 m high and 730 m long, and is the largest such structure in Europe. Several substantial reservoirs were created. The Fljótsdalur power station, situated over 400 m below ground level, has six 115 MW Francis turbines, has an installed capacity of 690 MW, and can generate up to 4,600 GWh. From here the electricity is sent through high voltage lines to the smelter, some 70 km distant.

Naturally, an impressive amount of tunnelling was necessary to divert water into penstocks to feed the power station. Impreglio used three new Robbins main beam gripper TMBs with diameters between 7.2 and 7,6 m diameter to penetrate the tough geological conditions, in conjunction with conveyors to remove spoil. In all 60.664 km of tunnels were bored, 48.046 km using the TMBs and 12.618 km using digging and boring. Work started in February 2003, tunnelling using the TMBs began late that year, and the final TMB breakthrough was on 9 April 2008, Impreglio completing its tunnelling activities in October that year.

With three of the four headrace tunnels, from Adits 1, 2 and 3, being 15.132 km, 10.275 km and 12.659 km in length respectively, Impreglio decided to build an underground rail network for the transport of materials and workers. A batch of 13 15-tonne diesel locomotives was ordered from GIA of Grängesberg (this concern was acquired by Atlas Copco in late 2011) in Sweden. Subsequently various machines (with interesting histories) were acquired from Schöma. With round-the-clock shift systems, the network was extremely busy, with three trains in continuous service.

In July 2004 the railway hit the international headlines for the wrong reason. A train carrying workers struck a cement mixer in the headrace tunnel under Valþjófstaðarfjall. Three people were injured. This is believed to have been the first ever rail accident involving passengers in Iceland. In July 2005 another Impreglio worker was injured in a train collision, this happening also in the main headrace tunnel.

In summer 2006 environmentalists staged protests at the various dam construction sites and at the aluminium smelter, security was stepped up, and understandably, Impregio tightened up on photography, visits, and releasing information. Very few news reporters managed to gain access to the site, the Italian company fearing that only environmentalists wanted to go there, to protest!

In 2013 a team of engineers from Schöma visited Iceland, and was able to clarify, to a certain extent, what material had been used at Kárahnjúkar.

The GIA Type DHD-15 locomotives had works numbers 1518 to 1527 (built 2004) and 1536 to 1538 (built 2006), and probably carried the fleet numbers 1 to 13.

Schöma Type CFL 180DCL, works number 5064, was built in 1990 for Transmanche Link for use during the construction of the English end of the Channel Tunnel. In 1994 it was used on Line 2 (east) of the München U-Bahn, then in 2001 on the Westerschelde tunnel project, then inserted in the 800 m deep Sedrun shaft of the Gotthard Base Tunnel for use during boring, before in 2006 being moved to Kárahnjúkar. In 2008 it was active in the 6.9 km Finne tunnel on the Erfurt to Leipzig high speed line. In 1998 it may even have visited Singapore for use on the metro.

Schöma Type CFL 180DCL, works numbers 5176 and 5177, were built in 1991 for Transmanche Link, which used them at the French end of the Channel Tunnel. In 1994 they were rebuilt by Schöma, and then used on the early stages of the Gotthard Base Tunnel before being moved to Austria in 1996 for use during the boring of the Semmering pilot tunnel. They were based at Kárahnjúkar in 2006, and in 2009 were in Russia, at Sochi during the reconstruction and doubling of the Black Sea coast main line.

Schöma Type CFL 180DCL, works number 5181 was built in 1991, for use on the French side of the Channel Tunnel. Its career was identical to the previous two, but it was not used on the Gotthard Base Tunnel, moving from the Schöma works to the Semmering pilot tunnel in 1995.

Schöma Type CFL 180DCL, works number 5214, built in 1991, worked on the French section of the Channel Tunnel, then in 1994 was rebuilt by Schöma, before being used from 1995 on the Semmering pilot tunnel. In 2007 it was moved to Kárahnjúkar, and after the dismantling of the rail network was plinthed on a short stretch of track near the HEP station.

Schöma Type CFL 180DCL, works number 5214, built in 1991, plinthed at Kárahnjúkar.

*Author's Collection*

# GREENLAND

A Schoema diesel at the quayside in Ivigtut in July 1980.

*Gunnar W. Christensen*

A large island, or rather, a large group of islands, the pioneer to manage a 'Grexit' from the EU, and whose mineral wealth resulted in an interesting assortment of railways, Kalaallit Nunaat is what the Inuits call Greenland, or Grønland, which is still part of the Kingdom of Denmark.

This 2.18 million km² territory, of which 419,500 km² (rapidly increasing) are ice-free and hence becoming ever greener in summer, is closer to Canada than to continental Europe. In 1972 Denmark and Greenland entered the EU, Greenland managing a 'Grexit' in 1985 following a disagreement over EU fishing regulations, and further autonomy from Denmark was voted for in a referendum on 25 November 2008. The currency remains, however, the Danish Krone, and possession of Greenland makes Denmark the 12th largest country in the world! 88% of Greenland's 56,500 inhabitants are of Inuit rather than European origins. Of the 150 km of roads, 60 km are asphalted, and of the 18 airstrips, 14 are asphalted. Most transport between settlements (all are on the coast) is by either air or, on the more hospitable west coast, by coastal shipping services, operated by the Arctic Umiaq Line (a sort of mini-Hurtigruten between Qeqertarsuaq in the north, Nuuk and Qaqortoq in the south). The capital town is Nuuk (formerly Godthåb or Godthaab, population 17,300), which

has its own municipal bus service, its 16 buses carrying over 2 million passengers in 2012. Under 14% of the population lives in 'rural' areas. Mining and fishing prompted the construction of the various railways known to have existed in mineral-rich Greenland.

## Qoornoq – fish on wheels

Qoornoq is on the northeast coast of the west coast island of Qoornuup Qeqertarsua in Nuup Kangerlua fjord, about 50 km north of Nuuk. The site of Qoornoq is believed to have been inhabited from paleo-Eskimo, pre-Inuit times, possibly as long ago as 2200 BC. Archaeological investigations have revealed traces of Norse buildings, from the tenth century colonisation. In the 1950s the settlement developed as a fishing community, and built various drying racks and sheds. There were hopes of this activity expanding substantially, so a short 600 mm gauge railway was laid between these buildings and the quay. Some sources suggest that the four-wheel platform wagons used on this line were hand-propelled, as was the case on railways on many Icelandic quaysides. Others reckon that a small diesel-hydraulic locomotive was used. The railway was operational between 1955 and 1971, and is still intact.

The railway used for the transport of fish at Qoornoq.

*Rachel E. Cotterill*

While the last permanent residents left Qoornoq in 1972, the village is still inhabited in summer, the railway having become something of a tourist attraction.

## Qullissat (Qutdligssat)

However no fewer than 26 diesel locomotives are known to have been used on railways in Greenland! Most of these could be found at Qullissat, on the north coast of Disko (Qeqertarsuaq) island, halfway up the west coast, where there were coal mines, and a substantial rail network. The coal measures here were known about for a long time, and initially exploited for local use.

In 1924 the Danish State decided to develop the mines on a large scale, to supply the whole of Greenland with its own fuel. No proper quays were built, so the coal had to be loaded into lighters to be moved to ships moored offshore. It was reckoned that between 400 and 500 tonnes could be loaded per day, with working taking place round the clock. Just north of the coal mine a large town, with close on 1,400 inhabitants, the foreign miners including Danes, Swedes and British, the sixth largest settlement in Greenland, evolved. The coal was not only sold to the domestic market, but was also exported to Denmark. At nearly 70ºN, the adjacent Baffin Bay was only ice-free from early May to early October, though mining continued year-round, the fuel being stockpiled in winter for sale in the spring.

There were two mine adits, roughly 20 m above sea level. One was served by a single 600 mm gauge track, the other by double track. These tracks fed a discharge installation, the coal being deposited on a lower level, whence a metre gauge track ran out above the quay, where there was a chute for loading the coal into the barges.

The mining started to become unprofitable after the Second World War, and in 1968, in spite of annual coal output having reached 40,000 tonnes in 1966, both the Danish Government and Grønlands Landsråd (the country's administrative body between 1908 and 1979) decided to put an end to operations. Profits were dwindling, and the coal was of poor quality. Closure came on 4 October 1972. By then over 700 residents had left the town, and the remaining 500 were then compulsorily relocated. On 20 October the town was sold to a private contractor, who demolished most of the buildings, though the wooden church was spared, being dismantled carefully in 1974 and moved to Jacobshavn (Ilulissat), where it was re-erected. The rail infrastructure was left intact, but . . .

In November 2000 a landslide on the opposite (northern) shore of Vaigat (Sullorsuaq Strait) created a tidal wave, estimated to be about 28 m high, which struck the north coast of Disko near Qullissat, levelling much of what then remained, including the railway. Sections of wrecked track remain, one of the rails dated 1915, and there are also various rusting mine tubs.

The early motive power (if any) for the rail network is unknown, and photographic records reveal nothing. Quite possibly manpower was used for moving mine tubs. In the 1950s and 1960s a batch of seven Type LBU two-axle diesel shunters was acquired by the Grønlands Tekniske

Two views of the derelict coal mining system at Qullissat on Disko Island.

*Klaus Bodholt Andreasen*

Organisation from Ruston & Hornsby's Waterside South works in Lincoln. These were:

| Works number | Year |
| --- | --- |
| 393338 | 1956 |
| 404971 | 1956 |
| 427803 | 1958 |
| 452291 | 1960 |
| 466583 | 1961 |
| 476113 | 1962 |
| 497732 | 1963 |

Following closure of the mines, all these were scrapped on site, in or around 1972.

## Den Sorte Engel (The Black Angel) of Mårmorilik

Mårmorilik is situated on the west coast of Greenland, in Qaasuitsup municipality, just to the north of Disko island. The mines (lead and zinc) are situated 24 km northeast of Ukkusissat on the mainland, on the eastern shore of Affarlikassaa fjord, a short arm running south from Qaumarujuk Fjord. 'Den Sorte Engel' refers to an angel-shaped exposed stratum of pelite on the marble cliffs on the eastern side of the fjord. The quality of the marble was considered to be as good as that from the more well-known

An unusual view of the cable car line at Mårmorilik, showing the two pairs of mine adits., to the right of which can be seen the 'Black Angel'.

*Gunnar W Christensen*

The original cable cars at Mårmorilik, in 1974.

*Author's Collection*

quarries at Carrara in Italy.

Mining started in or around 1938, continuing until 1945, the objective being to excavate blocks of marble, thus giving the mining settlement its name, Mårmorilik. The opencast quarrying took place on the western shore of Affarlikassaa fjord, close to sea level, and the blocks were moved from the workings by a 600 mm gauge railway, to the head of a double track inclined plane, which descended to the quay, where there was a further stretch of double track. Photos from this first mining era show loaded wagons being hand-shunted on the quay.

Marble quarrying led to the discovery of the Sorte Engel lead and zinc seams on the opposite (eastern) side of Affarlikassaa fjord, with explorations being undertaken by Danish geologists in the 1930s and 1940s. During the 1960s commercial investigations were realised by the Canadian firm Cominco, resulting in the formation in 1971 of a joint-venture between the Danish mining concern Greenex (37.5%) and Cominco subsidiary Vestgron Mines (62.5%). The joint-venture then obtained a 25-year mining concession. Exploitation started in 1973, 8,000 tonnes of lead concentrate and 46 000 tonnes of zinc concentrate being produced. Sales of 336 million DKK were achieved in 1974, when net earnings were 76 million DKK. That was precisely when prices for lead and zinc were starting to take off, so investment was thus quickly repaid. However, during the 1980s the price of metals started falling, a major loss was incurred in 1985, and the following year Cominco sold the mine to Boliden Mineral, which remained active until 1990 by cutting operating costs and workforce (the latter from 335 in late 1984 to 250 in late 1987). The peak year for production was 1979 (45,000 tonnes of lead and 151,000 tonnes of zinc). Mining ceased on 25 July 1990, and Greenex was liquidated in 1995, the Black Angel having yielded 590,000 tonnes of lead and 2,327,000 tonnes of zinc, generating sales of 1.154 billion DKK.

The transport arrangements for this second era of mining involved a 5 km 600 mm gauge line within the mountainside adit, just over 600 m above sea level. This fed a chute descending into an ore crusher, from which the minerals were loaded into 12 ten-tonne skips on one of two 1,500 m long (without any intermediate supports) parallel cableways, which ran from the adits (two pairs of narrow slits in the mountainside, one pair above the other) across the fjord to the fine ore bin in Mårmorilik, where there was also an ore mill. Two of the skips were fitted with cabins to carry miners to and from their shifts. The other cableway was used to transport materials required in the mine, and served the two adits at a higher level, above the ore crusher. In high winds blowing off the Greenland Ice Cap it was impossible to use the cableway – the miners being literally stranded in the mine workings, with only liquid refreshments. Haulage on the mine railway was provided by a fleet of six Clayton diesels, four built in 1972, two of an unknown date, and works numbers unknown, the mineral being moved from the working areas to the line by lorries. Following closure of the mines most of the buildings at sea level were demolished, the cableway dismantled, and sources of heavy metal contamination were cleaned up. The infrastructure within the mine adits remained largely intact.

A 1987 film of the mining activities can be found on:
https://www.youtube.com/watch?v=yyzzbtxKv4l

In 2007 the Greenland Government decided to revive the mines, to provide local employment, and a useful activity for the new airport at Qaarsut. Sales of zinc and iron ore would counter-balance the lump-sum subsidies received by Greenland from Denmark. Responsibility for reopening the mines was entrusted to Angel Mining (formerly Angus & Ross), registered in Britain, which in autumn 2007 took delivery of two new passenger-carrying cable cars to provide access to the adits and enable exploratory drilling to take place. By 2010 the narrow mine entrances in the almost sheer mountainside were being widened to 300 m, with prospects of restarting the workings in 2013, employing around 110 people. The mine was reckoned to have an economic lifespan of around 50 years, yielding both lead and zinc. However all this activity took place against a background of falling zinc prices from record high levels to their historic averages, and the mining project was shelved in 2013.

## Ivigtut

Situated in southwest Greenland near Kap Desolation, the name of this abandoned mining village translates as 'a grassy place', and is one of the very few places in the world where cryolite ($Na_3AlF_6$) or sodium aluminium fluoride, an important agent in the extraction of modern aluminium, can be found. The village could have been founded by Norse settlers as early as 985, and was then permanently inhabited until at least the 14th century. The cryolite deposits were discovered in 1799, the British engineer J. W. Tayler endeavouring to make use of the silver content, then giving up because it was too low for economic exploitation. Danish mining started in 1856, 53 tonnes being sent to København that year. In 1864 the Kriolit Mine og Handels Selskabet was granted a mining concession. From 1870 the main user was the Øresunds Chemiske Fabrikker.

The demand for cryolite increased radically following the creation of the Hall-Heroult Process, to improve the extraction of aluminium from bauxite ore. Production at Ivigtut then increased steadily, with exports to the USA starting, reaching 50,000 tonnes per annum in the 1920s. The outbreak of the Second World War resulted in the USA exports taking off, and was one of the reasons behind the latter country occupying Greenland, the US Army taking over responsibility for the defence of Ivigtut, and building fortifications in the district. Production reached a record 80,000 tonnes in 1943, and the same year US forces built Narsarsuaq airport. The cryolite was of course exported by ship.

Originally, mineral was removed from the opencast mine by means of a double track inclined plane, access for miners being via a series of wooden steps. Subsequently mine galleries were driven, and in 1949 a road tunnel was bored, to enable extraction using lorries, the surface portal being 500 m east of Ivigtut. During the 1960s production was reduced at the mines, and a crushing installation was built for sorting stockpiled cryolite. A heliport was built in nearby Grønnedal in 1971.

In 1982 the opencast workings, which had flooded after the start of underground mining, were drained, so that the last remaining cryolite on the quarry floor could be recovered. The mines were closed definitively in 1987, since synthesised cryolite was by then available, and in 2000 the last two families left Ivigtut for new houses in Grønnedal.

The rail network, 600 mm gauge, linked the inclined

One of the Schoema diesels at the quarry at Ivigtut in July 1980.

*Gunnar W. Christensen*

An ex-Ivigtut Schoema on display at the Hedelands Veteranbane west of København.

*Leif Jørgensen via Wikimedia Commons*

plane with the various factory buildings and the quay, the cryolite being moved in tubs. In the mid-1920s a lift, built using scaffolding techniques, supplemented the inclined plane. Haulage was provided originally by manpower, and then by three type CDL28 two-cylinder Deutz (28HP) Schöma V diesel tractors, one of which, built in April 1962, at the Krupp-Dolberg works, factory number 2649, was moved to Denmark in 1987 and the following year acquired by the HVB (Hedelands Veteranbane) for preservation. 2648 built in the same month and year, is also on the HVB. The third machine was 2647, also from 1962, whose fate is unknown.

## Josva

Between 1907 and 1914 Grønlandsk Minedrifts Aktieselskab (GMA) was involved in copper mining on the Josva peninsula in the appropriately named Kobbermine Bugt (Bay), near Innatsiaq. The company made use of a fleet of motor launches for local communications between the mining area and Qaqortoq (Julianehåb), and acquired the steamship *Danmark*, which had previously been used on a Danish expedition to northeast Greenland between 1906 and 1908, for the movement of materials and ore transport to and from continental Europe. Crude ore, cleaned by hand sorting of impurities, was shipped to Germany until 1911, when a smelter was built in Josva, enabling the ore to be refined until it had a 20% copper content. That year 500 tonnes of smelted copper were sent to the NKT Trådværket copper electrolysis factory, producing electric wiring, in Middelfart, Denmark.

The mining community was also dependent on raw materials brought in from the outside world, to enable smelting to take place. Coal was necessary, as were fluxes such as lime and pyrite, both imported from Scandinavia. Between 1911 and 1913 1,295 tonnes of copper ore were smelted, producing 93 tonnes of copper matte, or 19 tonnes of pure copper. Access to the mines was via a steep, 88m deep inclined shaft. There were five levels of working, involving the boring of 490 galleries, together with a number of 10 m deep test boreholes. The levels below 50 m were prone to flooding with seawater. There were 250 m of hardcore roads, and well over 500 m of narrow gauge railway network, linking the interior of the mine adits, the crusher, ore dressing trays, smelter and quays. Tubs were man-handled.

Josva village, consisted of 16 scattered buildings, many of which were of modular construction, a technique which by the early 20th century was becoming commonplace in Greenland, while the oldest building were of stone. Concrete was also used in construction. In 1913 a diesel generator was installed at the mining village to provide electricity, the settlement thus being one of the best equipped and up to date mining communities in Greenland.

However the copper lode failed to live up to the expectations of the early surveys, and both quantity and quality were lacking. The result was closure of the mine in 1914, the GMA incurring a loss of several million DKK. 2,252 tonnes of copper ore had been mined in around a decade, yielding just over 60 tonnes of copper. Over 50 kg of silver and 500 g of gold were also extracted. There is unlikely to be much copper ore remaining for extraction nowadays. Following the end of mining activities most of the modular and wooden buildings were dismantled and moved to nearby Ivigtut or Amitsoq.

## Amitsoq

This mixed opencast/underground graphite exploitation, on an island 15 km north of Nanortalik, was worked by the GMA between 1911 or 1914 and 1924, yielding around 6,000 tonnes of ore, with an average concentration of 20% of graphite, which was sent to København for final processing. The GMA moved the necessary buildings and equipment to Amitsoq from Josva. Infrastructure included a railway, probably 600 mm gauge, and tubs, with haulage provided by manpower.

Today the estimated reserves of graphite are 250,000 tonnes – a concession awaiting exploitation by bold venturers.

## Mestersvig

Mestersvig, an arm of Kong Oscars Fjord, is around 270 km north of Ittoqqortoormiit (Scoresbysund), at 72°10'N, and was named after the chief engineer on board the first steamship expedition to explore this area, in 1899. Extensive sea ice in the area means that shipping can only access Mestersvig for between four and eight weeks in summer. The Arctic night lasts two months, and permafrost lies to a depth of around 100 m.

In 1948 an expedition led by the Danish geologist Lauge Koch (1892 to 1964) on board the steamship *Gustav Holm*, discovered veins of galena-bearing quartz on the mountainsides to the northwest of Mestersvik, the main locations being Blyklippen and Sortebjerg. Lauge Koch returned in the summers of 1949, 1950 and 1951, and in 1952 Nordisk Mineselskab, a joint venture between the Danish state (27.5%), Boliden Mining (15%), Stora Kopparberg (15%), the Canadian Ventures (25%) and two private Danish concerns (15%), was founded with a capital of 15 million DKK to continue exploration and to exploit the lead/zinc strata at Blyklippen. The concession area covered around 100,000 km2, and mining and exploration rights were granted for 50 years.

A 12 km road was built from the quay at Nyhavn to the mine adit, and an airport with a 1,800 m long runway was built. Three adits were driven into the mountainside, at altitudes of 455, 415 and 335 m, totalling about 2,500 m in length. It was concluded that some 560,000 tonnes of ore, with concentrations of 11.1% lead and 8.6% zinc, awaited exploitation. This was insufficient for commercial exploitation, but the Danish State provided a loan, to get the project off the ground.

This really was a pioneering project. There was no infrastructure ready for use, the environment was harsh, the climate almost impossible. The processing mill (crushers, grinders, flotation trays, thickeners, filters and drying furnaces) and diesel power plant and air compressors all were located underground, at a depth below the 120 m of permafrost. The mill had a daily throughput capacity of 350 tonnes of ore. In a ten-month production run, about 90,000 tonnes of ore could be dealt with. Pre-heated water had to be used for drilling in frozen rock. Granby dump cars were used on the 415 m level (the main one) to move the ore to the crushing installations. Once the concentrate had been obtained, it was compressed into large blocks, of either 4 tonnes of lead concentrate or 2.5 tonnes of zinc concentrate. Road transport was used for transport to the quay at Nyhavn, the blocks being store on pallets in the open to await shipment

KALAALLIT NUNAAT

*Mestersvig-imi aqerlussarsiorfik, 1956-63*
*Blyminen ved Mestersvig, 1956-63*

GRØNLAND 10.00

Ina Rosing fec. 2014

A Danish/Greenlandic Post Office issue showing a train at Mestersvig.

*Klaus Bodholt Andreasen*

to Antwerpen and Bremerhaven during the brief summer, the Danish shipping company J. Lauritzen having won the contract, and using its fleet of new 'Polar' cargo ships with ice-strengthened hulls. The mines were inactive in December and January, used for staff holidays.

The rail network was 750 mm gauge. Part of it was on the 415 m level, and part on the 335 m level and partly situated in the open air, presumably serving a loading installation for lorries. The evidence for this comes from a 10.00 DKK Greenlandic stamp issued in 2014, showing one of the four Ruston & Hornsby Type LB diesel tractors, built by Waterside South works in Lincoln, with a rake of 11 Granby dump cars. This would appear to be a colour photo, rather than a painting. The machines were:

| Works number | Year |
| --- | --- |
| 398105 | 1956 |
| 402610 | 1957 |
| 404978 | 1957 |
| 427814 | 1958 |

Between 1955 and 1962 the mines yielded 544,600 tonnes of mineral, of which 9.3% was lead, 9.9% zinc, and the remainder spoil. Mining ceased in late 1962. Following closure the diesel generators were removed from their underground chamber, while two of the Claytons, 398105 and 402610, had been transferred in 1960 for use at the nearby Malmbjerget Molybdæn mine. In 1974 the barrack buildings at Blyklippen which were in the best state were moved to Nyhavn to establish a new exploration base, and in 1983 all but two of the remaining buildings were burned, as part of a cleaning up operation. A significant stretch of shoreline was also affected by pollution from the washing of ore, while there were instances on which large numbers of canvas sacks containing concentrate were dropped accidentally into the sea at Nyhavn.

## Malmbjerget Molybdæn

The 1750 m high Malmbjerg ('Ore Mountain') is situated on the east coast, at 72°N, some 25 km south of Blykippen. The molybdenum deposit here was discovered in 1954 by members of the Danish East Greenland Expeditions, during mapping of the area. Nordisk Mineselskab undertook further exploration between 1955 and 1961, and in 1962 entered into a joint venture with American Metal Climax (from 1974 AMAX). The origins of 'Climax'? The molybdenum deposit discovered in 1879 in Colorado, near Climax railway station at the summit of the Continental Divide, on the line from Denver to Leadville!

At Malmberg three adits, totalling 1,329 m in length, were driven, and a body of ore was encountered. However it was deemed that prices were too low for mining to be economically viable, given the size of the mineral reserves – an estimated 119 million tonnes with a molybdenum concentration of just 0.25%. The old joint venture was disbanded, and a new one, with the same partners, created in 1979. Drilling for deep ore, using a 972 m drill hole, proved negative, and AMAX withdrew from the joint venture. Mineral exploration was abandoned in 1984, and efforts were concentrated on oil exploration further south in Jameson Land, until Nordisk Mineselskab was liquidated in 1991. The eventual fate of the Ruston & Hornsby diesel tractors is unknown. Perhaps one or two are still languishing in the abandoned adits, together with the rest of the machinery?

In 2004 the mining concession was acquired by Galahad Gold, which late that year founded International Molybdenum (InterMoly) as the sole stakeholder, conducting new surveys the following year, envisaging that the mine could supply around 4% of total global demand for molybdenum. The latest concession-holder, Malmbjerg Molybdenum, planned to start up exploitation in 2011, using a workforce of 600 to prepare the site and a mining team of 400 over the coming 20 years to extract the metal. The price of molybdenum had reached a record level by 2005, thus encouraging the project, but by 2008 had fallen back to its long term average.